GOOD SELLING!

PAUL H. GREEN

THE GREEN SHEET, INC.

Published by The Green Sheet, Inc., Rohnert Park, CA.

Published in the United States by The Green Sheet, Inc.

http://www.greensheet.com

ISBN 0-9670947-0-4

Cover: Original oil painting by Paul H. Green, *Fragile Light.*
Photographed by Tiffany Lucas

Text design by Julie O'Ryan-Dempsey

Cartoons appearing on pages 6, 13, 33, 44, 53, 60, 94, 101, 131, 142 by Bradford Veley, Marquette, MI.

Manufactured in the United States of America, R.R. Donnelley & Sons Company, Book Publishing Services.

First Edition: May 1999
10 9 8 7 6 5 4 3 2 1

What others are saying about Good Selling!

"Two of life's greatest mysteries are: Why do 20% of salespeople sell 80% of the goods and services? Why do some banks never seem to make a bad loan and others do?

Paul Green goes a great job of addressing the first question. Good Selling is a comprehensive review of what it takes to be in the top 20% of salespeople. Its lessons are worth revisiting for all salespeople. Now, if only he would write a companion book on banking."

Brandes Elitch, Vice President
National Bank of the Redwoods

"Mr. Green, I wanted to let you know that I just finished your new book Good selling. I think it is SUPERB! I am going to make it required reading for all existing and over 350 new employees annually. I will also provide the book to ISOs, banks, and our business partners. Thank you for providing such quality reading."

J. David Siembieda, EVP Sales & Marketing
CrossCheck, Inc.

"Paul Green's ability to create a workable selling approach for payment services is a gift to any person wishing to make a career in the portfolio building business. Both industry veterans and neophytes should invest their time to read this book if they wish to improve their production or gain more enjoyment from their work."

Robert O. Carr, CEO
Heartland Payment Services

"Once again you have broken new ground in this industry by offering the person on the street a guide that can do nothing but help them to put more money in their pocket.

Paul, your knowledge of this industry shines through with these helpful sales tips and advice. I am always being asked by ISOs for a sales guide to help them train sales people. I now have one that I can send them."

Dan Lewis, Vice President
American National Bank of DeKalb County

"With over 30 years of sales experience, I find Good Selling! a beginning sales primer or a great refresher for an experienced sales professional."

Ken Boody, CEO
The Horizon Group

"This is a book you can open to any page and receive immediate value. . .whether you're a veteran sales pro or a rookie. What a wonderful contribution to the Payment System Industry and to the sales profession. Good Selling! is a book that could become required reading for all of us involved in the sales process. . .and who isn't?"

Terry R. Stoupa, EVP Sales & Marketing
CellGate Technologies LLC

"As an executive in a number of sales firms I have always yearned for general sales support books. Most of the books were written from an "ivory tower" approach and would be seen as a joke to most sales people because of the theoretical review of the subject. Your book has captured the "Street Savvy" that most salespeople need to know in mastering their art. In Good Selling! you have distilled hard won experience into a step by step approach to selling with tips and motivation usually only found in high priced seminars."

Brian K. Roemmele, President
Multiplex Media Corp.

"Not since Og Mandino's *The Greatest Secret in the World* has a book so recognized the moral imperative of the selling profession. At the same time, this book goes beyond inspiration to how too's, not only of sales profession, but the how too's of business success. Move over Dale Carnegie, there is a new kid on the block named Paul Green, and his book provides the skills needed to succeed in approaching the 21st Century."

Myles F. Suer, President
Personal Solutions Corporation

Acknowledgments

I owe a special debt of gratitude to all the sales professionals I have worked with through the years, and who have helped me to have such a rich life. Within the covers of this book I try to show the admiration I feel for the profession and the respect I have for people who must struggle daily in this noble and difficult occupation.

I would also like to make certain acknowledgments in connection with writing this book. No job in my life has ever been accomplished without assistance from others and this has been no exception. I wish to thank Julie O'Ryan-Dempsey and Suzanne Cagnassola for their most significant contributions to *Good Selling!*

I wish to thank Dr. Juanita Chamberlain as well, for her editing and insightful comments, and with the stroke of her red pen helped me to hold my split infinitives to a minimum.

Finally, I wish to thank my wife, Tischa, and our children and grandchildren for their patience and understanding.

Forward

Good *Selling!* is written as a tool for sales professionals and Independent Sales Organizations (ISOs) working in the Financial Services Industry. While this book outlines the basics from Getting Organized to Presentations and Closing, it has practical advice for beginners and reminders for those of us who have been selling for some time.

The sale of financial services and the birth of thousands of sales positions in the industry since 1983 has been of great benefit to equipment manufacturers as well as the banking and the credit card industry. As we approach the 21st century, the need for sales professionals in this area of commerce has never been greater. I hope this book will help those who receive it, and if you find it beneficial, please pass it on to someone else in need of the basics.

I use the concept of a sales professional needing to be "thick-skinned" several times in this book. I realize that this expression can have negative connotations and even conjure up negative stereotypes of a salesperson. In fact, I also use Willie Loman-like images in several places, and even close with a quote from Arthur Miller. I hope each reader will understand the overall direction of the advice. I know that most of us don't want to face rejection and not let it bother us; but rather want to see concrete reasons why rejection is not the point. In fact, most of us don't really want to grow "thick skins" and (like Willie Loman) grow so oblivious to insult that we are willing to sink to any level just to make a sale. In practice, and that **is** the point of this book, the difference is one between sales as attempted seduction and as the art of persuasion.

Today more and more women than ever before are in the sales profession, and some of the most successful sales professionals selling payment services are and have been women. However, many women and many men as well, abhor the Willie Loman image; in fact, they will go to extremes to contradict it. Unlike the Willie Lomans of the past, the sales professional today refuses to be offended if the prospect is in a bad mood or preoccupied, but not because they fear rejection. On the contrary, it is out of respect for his or her own authority as a Sales Professional. As a professional, they are aware that the moment they give in to personal offense, they give up their position as expert and problem solver, along with any influence they may have excised over the prospect.

I wish to make one more point to the reader before you begin this book. Please read the quotation from *Death of a Salesman* with the irony it deserves. In my opinion, Arthur Miller despised the sales profession almost as much as he despised puritans, without understanding either one.

I hope everyone reading this book will understand that nothing happens in this country until some salesperson sells it. The overall message of this book is one of hope, confidence, and belief in oneself and one's ideals. These are the makings of not only successful sales professionals, but happy human beings.

Good Selling!

Paul H. Green

Chapter 1

Introduction

Fortune Finds Those Who Look for It

I always find it refreshing to talk to ISOs and individual sales representatives about their perspective of what is happening on the street. This is one of the reasons I spend several days each year conducting proactive phone interviews, in addition to responding to the calls I regularly receive. One thing that strikes me with every conversation is that it takes a special breed of individual to be a salesperson. Those who are really successful make their own breaks.

If I had my life to live over again, I would elect to be a trader of goods rather than a student of science. I think barter is a noble thing.
—Albert Einstein

Sales, of course, is not for everyone. Not all who call themselves salespeople actually are. Some people in sales act like sparrows sitting in the nest with their mouths open, squealing and waiting for the next handout. That's okay for baby sparrows, because they are babies and they are helpless; but the lifetime player, who knows what it means to be a professional salesperson, knows handouts are not a strategy designed to create success—certainly not long term success!

I like the old joke about the mother who was having difficulty getting her son out of bed in the morning. "Mom," he was crying, "Why do I have to go to school today?" The mother replied, "For three reasons: First because it's Monday, second because I said so, and third because you're the principal."

Not a hilariously funny story, but what humor there is in it stems from the fact that this is not a little kid acting like a little kid; it's a grown-up. It's a lot less funny when you think of the number of people in the business world who have the same attitude as that school principal lying in bed in the morning. There comes a time in the growing process when you're no longer a sparrow in the nest or a little kid fighting against the sandman.

The secret of success in sales—and one of the secrets of achieving happiness and peace of mind in life—is to do what you can and all you can for yourself. In other words, make your own breaks. Do more than what others expect of you. Do more than your job demands. Don't depend on others. Don't depend on the company you represent to do things for you, albeit you still must go on the leads you're given. Support is a wonderful thing, but when it becomes a way of life, success (that is, long term personal achievement) can easily decline.

Winning in sales always results from the same simple process: hard work. Referrals or leads are nice, and interested prospects that call you out of the blue can make your day, but they are seldom a steady diet.

Regardless of whether you are knocking on doors or smiling and dialing, nothing replaces the hard work of starting all over again tomorrow.

On Being Independent

Being an "independent" sales representative has its perks, and most people don't think about them. Now I'm not sure that I really want the world to know how great this profession is, but I will tell you, and trust that you'll keep this secret just between us. For one thing, the reason I became a salesperson in the first place is that I realized I need more freedom than the average person does. That whole 9 to 5 thing, or tote that barge, lift that bale, is just plain silly. Well, at least for the weak of heart. But then those types don't become professional persuaders, do they?

I often hear from the "Persuasion Challenged" that they just can't imagine living a life of feast or famine. I always laugh to myself because this is exactly the reason I got into sales in the first place. You know it's **all** mountains and valleys. I love wandering through the valleys, and then tackling another mountaintop. The air is clean and fresh and there is always a challenge just up ahead. I decide when to run, and when to rest.

> *There is only one success ... to be able to spend your life in your own way, and not to give others absurd maddening claims upon it.*
> —*Christopher Morley*

Once I realized I liked the pace of a "sales professional," then I learned about "reping" products as an independent. It just seemed like a natural flow. I had always heard the terms, ISO, Independent Sales Representative, Value Added Reseller, Manufacturer's Rep. All these terms seemed somehow bigger, better descriptions of how I felt. They properly elevated my job and its value.

Of course until I cut the corporate strings, I didn't completely appreciate the perks, you know, like sleep when you need it. When I worked as a sales employee, my feet had to hit the floor at 5:30 A.M. if I was going to make a timely appearance at the morning sales meetings. And what the heck, I never was a breakfast type anyway. And that "raise my quota and change my territory" thing, what's up with that?

Now, while I indeed have to pay twice the level of social security tax as the employee sales reps I compete against, I decide when, where, and how I sell. Of course, I read the sales materials and recommendations of the marketing departments in the companies for whom I offer products or services; you have to, if you are going to know the latest lingo and the new widgets. I also attend a motivational class or two each year, although I don't think I got to one last year. And when I'm a little down, I call the sales support department of that great widget company in the West, and talk to that Karen lady. She is really great; I can talk to her anytime and for as long as I like, since her company pays her, after all, to talk to me.

Finally, when I am really gloating about the great job I have, I think about that no smoking in the office rule. Every time I see a bunch of office workers huddled in the breeze-way of some office building, I realize that it is this rule that is probably going to breed the next generation of entrepreneurs.

So, when I hear that another 50 heads are going to roll at "Perpetually Sincere Card Services," or it's another black Friday at "Just-In-Time Bankcard," I kind of enjoy it. I know it's wrong, but darn it, if you're going to take on self-employment, you're entitled to gloat, aren't you? Given the fact that I sometimes have to struggle to pay my bills on a slow month, have to remember to save during the best of times, can't remember what a paid vacation is, and often work seven days a week to get a large account all the support it deserves, I'm satisfied to know that at least I won't be downsized.

After all, I earn every nickel I make, and I decide when.

Cartoon by Bradford Veley, Marquette, MI

Chapter 2

Getting Organized

Getting the Most from Your Work Day

Are you all over the place in your workday? Do you start one project, then move to the next, never tying up anything? Are you driving from one end of town to another, sometimes going back to your office because you need contracts or other materials? Or, are you just the opposite? Do you stay with one task and see it through to the end, even if it conflicts with other opportunities?

> *Salespeople need an almost magical blend of planning, innovation, street smarts, and dedication.*
> *—John Gallagher*

Obviously, neither of these scenarios is ideal. Both work habits can interfere with your responsibilities and your ability to get sales. Try the following tricks to help you get the most out of your workday.

- Each morning, before you delve into your selling or paperwork tasks, decide what projects you're going to work on. Plan the order in which you will attack them and make sure you have all the names, phone numbers, back up, and supplies necessary. (If you're going on sales calls today, do you have a map and do you know where you are going?)

- As you work, focus on what you're doing **right now.** If you've organized your tasks effectively, you won't be interrupted by deadlines for other projects, call-backs, or missed opportunities.

- Learn to recognize when you've completed all you can on a particular project, including on initial sales calls. Your efforts may not be finished, but that's OK. Move on and insert the project or opportunity in your list, and mark when you think you will be able to accomplish more on it.

So take the time you need in the morning, even if it means going to work a little early or letting voice mail catch the phones. Just a few minutes can determine whether you have a good day or a bad one, if you make deadlines or miss them, and if you have closed sales or closed doors.

Getting Organized

In years past, the disorganized salesperson was easy to recognize: the cluttered desk or car, the stacks of paper, and the post-it-notes covering the calendar were all dead give-a-ways. Now that we've entered the information age, the PC or day planner has revolutionized the business world and solved all of our organizational problems. Right? Wrong! The disorganized person is now overwhelmed with managing disk-space and the reams of data in addition to all of the paper clutter. And if you're thinking that because you work alone as a salesperson, no one up above is going to ask you for anything you can't find, think again. Your existing customers and prospects expect that you will be organized.

> *Nothing succeeds like the appearance of success.*
> —*Christopher Lasch*

While time-management and project-management methods abound, organization processes or computers don't solve disorganization. These management tools work only if a system is in place. Here are twelve tips to organize your information flow and improve your information management skills:

1) Handle each piece of paper once. Don't set papers aside. Make the decision now; if it must wait, use a "tickler file." Ticklers only work, however, when checked daily for suspense items.

2) Sort mail with your wastebasket at your side. Don't let the junk mail monster eat your valuable time.

3) Take notes on notepads, not scraps. Full sheets of paper hold more information and can be filed with less risk of loss.

4) Use only one calendar! Mark all appointments in pencil.

5) Avoid labeling files as "Miscellaneous," "Information," or "Pending." These are vacuums that the business universe will fill.

6) Schedule time to read daily. Thirty minutes a day should keep you current with the never-ending stream of information you need to stay current in your sales skills and product knowledge.

7) Make sure your paper files match your electronic records. Your file-drawers should match your directory tree on your PC (assuming you have one); hence, you will know where to find your information in the office or in cyberspace.

8) Sort through your stacks of paper. Eliminate outdated, duplicate, or unnecessary information. Do you really need both the hardcopy and computer file of a document? Copy the file onto a labeled diskette and recycle the hardcopy.

9) Delete automatic back-up files. Many programs create backup copies of your documents automatically, and these double the disk space usage. Search for .BAK or .BKP files and delete them periodically.

10) Unused software programs waste hard-drive space. Delete the programs you no longer use. If you're running Windows programs, you may find it more efficient to use one of the "uninstall" programs that is available, in order to ferret out all of the files associated with a given program.

11) Clear out your hard-drive by archiving old files to diskettes. Make sure you label the diskettes, or you will have created another informational black hole that will sabotage your organization system.

12) File all equipment manuals and instructions in one place. Write the serial numbers for your software programs inside the cover of the user's manual and on a Rolodex® card with the support line phone number.

Once you've imposed order to the chaos of your life, you will be more efficient. By staying organized, you can devote more time to selling and less time to finding things.

Keep Learning

In many professions, continued training, updates, and brush-ups are required for continued certification. However, many who have perfected their selling skills to become professional sales executives are reluctant to put themselves in the learning role.

We should all recognize that we can get better at what we do. Even for those of us who have proven themselves in this profession, a fresh look at the basics can generate new ideas and reinforce our strengths.

A story reported by the *London Daily Record* says it another way: "Lucky, a German shepherd guide dog, will be retrained and given to a new blind owner."

"Lucky led his first owner in front of a moving bus, and the second off the end of a pier," new trainer Ernst Gerber told the newspaper. "He actually pushed his third owner off a railway platform just as the Cologne-to-Frankfurt express was approaching, and he walked his fourth owner into heavy traffic before running away to safety."Gerber said Lucky is "a damned good guide dog. He just needs to brush up on some elementary skills."

"While you're young, your job is to download and store as much data as possible, no matter how strange some of it seems. Then, one day, you'll realize that a very cool utility program called 'wisdom' has interlaced with your operating system, and BINGO! Life will make a lot more sense!"

Cartoon by Bradford Veley, Marquette, MI

Chapter 3

Staying Motivated

You Motivating You!

Keeping yourself motivated can be your most challenging job. Here are some tips that will help:

Establish a support group. Whether it's your office mates or e-mail pals, connect yourself with other sales professionals you can rely on for assistance, counsel, and critique. With cellular phones, the Internet, and faxes, even the most isolated salesperson can establish a "team." I know of two people who called each other each morning at 6:45 to recite a motivational poem. It took one minute out of their morning and set the tone for their entire day.

> *Everyone who is truly successful in sales has learned to overcome rejection, and to remember every day: SW, SW, SW, N!*
>
> *Some Will, Some Won't, So What, Next!*
>
> *—Unknown*

Turn off the radio! Listening to the radio in the morning is a sure way to bring yourself down. The mornings are filled with bad news you can't change, and if something really important happens you'll find out about it soon enough. Instead, use your commute time to listen to motivating tapes and positive messages. Most video rental businesses and libraries have a selection of audiotapes you can rent or borrow. Try listening to Tom Hopkins, Zig Ziglar, Og Mandino, Robert Schuller or even Shirley MacLaine to start your morning on an upbeat note.

Keep your perspective! In 100 years, will anyone remember? Botched presentations, missed appointments, customer problems, and innumerable business stresses really aren't the end of the world. Remember to take a moment to look at the big picture and today's small place in it. Don't let the challenges you face become bigger than they actually are.

Take a break! Get outside at least once a day. Taking a lunch break is actually more productive than working through lunch. Give your mind a break and gain a fresh perspective.

Review your goals and rewards! If your idea of success is a cherry 1967 Mustang, put a picture of one on your desk or bathroom mirror. List your short-term and long-term goals, and post this list by your desk with the heading "I Will!" As you review the list, visualize yourself having attained your goals. Plan your day with these goals in mind. If the task in front of you doesn't lead to one of your goals, don't go there—perhaps someone else needs that job.

Use those Post-its®! Leave yourself little "at-a-boys (girls)." "I sold five accounts today!" "My residual income increased today!" "Happiness is a positive cash flow!" (My personal favorite) "25 days 'til Mexico!" Be sure to leave yourself notes on Friday afternoon to find on Monday morning—they'll probably surprise you!

On the Virtues of Being Positive

If you say things to yourself such as, "That account doesn't want to see me," or "They'll never call me back," or "They're not going to sign with me," then you're absolutely right, they won't.

But if you say, "I'm going to get that sale. I'll ask why they think it's too expensive and show them why they need to buy," or "I'll call them and be sure to follow up," you will change the outcome of the situation.

> *Positive anything is better than negative nothing.*
> *—Elbert Hubbard*

What's the difference between these two scenarios? Attitude. The difference between a good and bad attitude isn't that one is sweet and the other surly. People with healthy perspectives know that they have the power to change situations. They also know that no matter how bad a situation is, it is only temporary.

A person with a bad attitude believes that conditions are permanent, beyond their control, and they have no choice but to accept them.

You have the power to change your situation simply by changing your perspective. Everything has a cause and an effect. If you don't like the effect, identify the cause and change it. For example, if a prospect isn't returning your calls, don't tell yourself that there's nothing you can do. Instead, take the four steps that will put you back in charge:

1. Identify the effect (you haven't signed the account).

2. Identify the cause (the prospect didn't call you back).

3. Change the cause (call the prospect).

4. Change the effect (you keep the prospect as a contact and perhaps a customer, if not now, then in the future).

Don't give the power to others; you are the key to your own success.

There will be setbacks. The prospect still may not buy from you even though you followed up. But one day, if you stick with it long enough, you will make progress—maybe with that prospect, maybe with someone else.

Your attitude will determine how successful you are. By modifying your manner toward the people you deal with, the things you do, and life in general, you decide what happens.

Can't Means Won't

Did your mother ever say that to you? How about your coach or teacher? What they were trying to say (in their infinite wisdom) was that we are each our own worst enemy. Only we can prevent ourselves from achieving. And, if we determine we **can't** do something before we ever actually try, we are certain to fail.

Do you find yourself saying or thinking phrases such as, "I should do some research on the competition, but.."I can't take that computer class because. . .," "I would go visit that new merchant downtown if. . ."

The way to get out of these negative thoughts is to first determine what is preventing you from trying to achieve your goals, and no fair blaming someone or something else. For example, "They don't pay me enough," or "They don't give me enough control," or "If I were in charge..." Sound familiar? Try to figure out **why** you don't get it done, not **who** is preventing you from achieving.

Ask yourself: Is it fear? Are you so afraid you will fail that it's better to never try so no one can call you a failure? Is it laziness? Do you think the effort is just not worth the payoff? Is it discouragement? Did you try before and fail? Do you now believe it will be a wasted effort?

When you hear yourself saying, "won't" or "can't" or "but," find out what the real obstacle is. Finding out why you're limiting yourself can help you destroy those self-made barriers and go after what you want. What do you have to lose? Probably a lot less than you have to gain. Take a stab at it.

Be Successful...Stop Quitting!

> *Few things are impossible to diligence and skill ... Great works are performed, not by strength, but perseverance.*
>
> *—Samuel Johnson*

Why do we fail? Many times we don't really fail; we just think we fail because we don't meet our goal in the allotted time. In other words, we were either too tough on ourselves or our time clocks are really set badly. But, if our deadline isn't realistic, it's not failure as much as it is bad timing. Make sure you have enough time to accomplish your goals; and if you need more, allow it.

EXAMPLE: Don't set a goal of becoming the company's top salesperson after your first year in the industry. Make that a goal for year two or three. Today, set a goal of 50 cold calls a day during the first month, and 10 sales. Set the next month's goal higher. If the top gun in your office does more, then plan to out-work him or her. The results you desire should follow.

So now you have two major elements: setting the goal and establishing the time frame. What's missing? You need a plan of action.

EXAMPLE: You may have set a mini-goal of getting an appointment with a big account in the next month. That's good. It's an achievable goal in a reasonable amount of time. But, do you know how you're going to a get that appointment? Are you going to call them? Great, but what if that doesn't work? What's plan B, send a letter? And C? To get that appointment you must have a plan (and alternates) such as networking, contacts, or tradeshows. Some goals take a lifetime! People who stick it out meet their goals more often than those who don't.

If you stop calling on the prospect who has refused to see you eight times, you're certain to fail. You'll never see them again so you certainly won't sell them. But, if you hang in a little longer, your chances of success are much greater. I was told by a *Green Sheet* reader that he succeeded in selling Big O Tires by explaining what others had not. He called on the account numerous times, and so had many others. In fact, the account had presentations from both Equifax Check Services and TeleCheck the week of his sale. However, with all these calls and companies, no one had ever mentioned a Multiple Check feature. Explaining how the ability to write more than one check could be beneficial to Big O won him the sale. Four checks for four tires sold the account. Persistence pays!

Consider Your Competitors Your Allies

What? Those people are my friends? You mean I have to take their photos and logo off my dartboard? Yes, your competitors are your allies, and they can help you increase your sales—even

> *The secret to creativity is knowing how to hide your sources.*
> *—Albert Einstein*

those ISOs you've lost accounts to. Competitors can kick-start your selling efforts by helping to establish a need for your service, motivating you to learn more, and adding spice to your daily selling efforts.

First, if a prospect chooses a competitor's service, a big part of your job is already completed—the need for your service has already been established. Now, all you must do is find out what made that prospect choose the other ISO or salesperson and how to get him/her to switch to you.

How? Ask the prospect. He or she is your best source for finding out how you can improve your work. The merchant may give you some hints as to the competitor's weaknesses too. Maybe the merchant initially believed the approval process would be a little easier, or perhaps the customer service department isn't as accessible as it should be. No one is perfect. But don't knock the competition; just let the merchant talk. In that way, your competitor has continued to aid you by providing exposure to fresh information and ideas.

So, the sale has gone to a competitor, you've picked up some hints from the prospect, now what? Well, move on to someone else, but check back with that merchant in a month or so. If things haven't worked out, you have left the door open by demonstrating that you're still interested in their business. Again, the competitor has helped you and their loss will be your gain.

Finally, your competitors can motivate you and add intrigue to your selling efforts. Just think how great you will feel when you finally sell that prospect who was being pursued by "The Competition."

Choose Your Own Destiny

Life is full of choices. Here or to go? Paper or plastic? Smoking or non-smoking? There are some other choices you make every day that you may not even be aware of. Did you choose to set up five presentations this week? Did you choose to sell two accounts today? These things aren't in your control, you say? Well, I say they are.

> *If you can dream it, you can do it.*
>
> *—Walt Disney*

Successful people don't rely on the magic of that "lucky" tie when calling on big accounts. They are people who are prepared, persistent, and positive. If you've been hoping for good fortune, it's not going to happen. You've got to make it happen.

How?

First, you have to know what you want, so that when you get it (and you will), you'll recognize it. Once you've figured out what you want from your selling efforts, you just have to **CASH** in.

Be **C**reative. Break free from the rules and think creatively. Make an effort with each call to do something new, even if the old way works just fine.

Assume the unexpected. When it happens, it won't be such a shock.

Become a **S**ponge. Take every opportunity to learn. It will give you confidence in yourself and increase other's confidence in you. Spend the time you're not working doing things that are educational and fun. Listen to National Public Radio; read a new trade publication; leave a story on the The Green Sheet "Tales of Sales Experience" hotline.

Say "**H**ello." Every person you meet is an opportunity. Always carry business cards to give to new acquaintances, and don't forget the acquaintances you already have. Work to maintain and rekindle relationships with friends, co-workers, and former classmates. It can mean referrals and leads. Use your time in restaurants and stores to build rapport with employees and owners.

CASH in on your own potential and expect the best. Think that you can and you will!

Fill 'er Up

Are you running low on creativity? Maybe you're still using a presentation that was created on papyrus. Or, maybe you keep to the same schedule every day, and the routine is becoming monotonous.

Get out of that slump! Reorganize your day. Take a new way to work. If you normally drive to work, take public transportation or bike for a day. Listen to a different radio station or turn off the radio completely. Move your office furniture around. Write a new sales script. Eat something you've never tried for lunch. If you usually drive to lunch, walk instead. If you regularly use your computer, pick up a pen and write for a while.

Simple changes in your daily activities can leave you with a new attitude that will transform you into a refreshed and rejuvenated sales professional.

Nothing Personal

Everyone knows you need a thick skin to make it in sales. While there are some "born sellers," not all of us are born with thick skins. We want people to like us. We want people to want to be around us. We want people to approve of our actions.

So does that mean that if we're sensitive we can't be successful sales professionals? Certainly not. If you weren't born with a thick skin there's still time to grow one! The key is to remember that when prospects reject your service or act indifferently, they are reacting to your product, not you.

For example, if a prospect says "No," that isn't necessarily a reflection of your selling skill. You represent your product; you are not the product. The rejection is aimed at the service, not you. Keep in mind that the service isn't for everyone, and move on.

Likewise, when it seems a merchant really couldn't care less about your presentation, keep in mind that your presentation may not be the most stimulating, but that doesn't mean you're boring. Work on making your presentation more interesting and refine your presentation skills, but remember it is just a presentation, it is not you.

Don't let rejection bully you into procrastinating calls or avoiding appointments. The best way to learn to deal with rejection is to face it head-on and remember, it's nothing personal.

"You" Can get You Your Next Sale

Next time you practice your presentation, record yourself on either audio or video. When you are finished, review the tape and note every time you say "I" or "We." Wherever possible, replace those instances with "You."

Instead of saying, "We offer a variety of Premium Services," replace it with, "You can benefit from Premium Approval, Visa/MasterCard Acceptance and the new "Widget" POS terminal. Which would you like to hear about first?"

> *A wise man will make more opportunities than he finds.*
>
> *—Francis Bacon*

Or instead of, "We've been in the business for 15 years and we know what companies like yours need," try "You're a competent business professional; tell me what a business such as yours needs to succeed."

Rather than saying, "We are the only company in this industry to offer programs customized for each merchant," how about saying, "If you could pick and choose only the coverage you need, would you?"

Take the emphasis off yourself and focus your presentation on the merchant and how your offering will work for him or her.

> *Sales is all about attitude. To prove the point, think about how many words and phrases there are for the word "quit":*
>
> *stop, terminate, disengage, cease, forsake, throw in the towel, resign, give-up, or take no for an answer.*
>
> *While there is really only one phrase for "success"... don't quit!*
>
> *—Me*

Six Steps to Success

Following these steps will lead you down the path to more and better sales.

1. Visualize yourself as a winner. Your positive self-esteem is essential to your success. Monitor your internal dialog carefully. Instead of telling yourself, "I'll never close this account," tell yourself, "I am a can-do sales person.

2. Solidify your goals. Write down and prioritize what you want to accomplish. Define the intermediate steps and short-term objectives between you and your desires. List these action items on your daily "to do" list.

3. Energize yourself by knowing where you're going and giving your all to getting there. Inventory your strengths and weaknesses, then design a plan to overcome those weaknesses that are preventing you from achieving your goals.

4. Lifelong learning is a hallmark of superachievers. Determine what additional knowledge and training you need to accomplish your goals. Seek out books, tapes, classes, and organizations that will give you what you need.

5. Develop a positive attitude. Problems, fears, and setbacks are facts of life. You can maintain a positive attitude by using motivational tapes and books, cultivating positive language, and learning to give yourself a break.

6. Never give up. Believe in yourself, your skills, and your product. Perseverance will ensure your success.

Following these six simple steps will enable you to formalize your sales goals and make them a reality.

Tending Your Sales Garden

While you're planting your spring vegetables and flowers, remember that it's also time to tend to your garden of sales skills and methods. With any garden or project you need a plan of desired results, a decision on which seeds to plant and where. Without a plan and the decision to carry it through, your garden will languish, and only the weeds will flourish. Without a sales plan, the weeds of negative thinking and laziness will overtake your garden of prospects.

As a Sales Professional, you need to nurture your garden of sales knowledge in order to harvest positive sales results (ongoing residuals). By planting new positive sales skills and ideas and tending your garden daily through positive self-talk and productive discipline, you will keep the weeds of negative thinking and laziness at bay.

Here is a simple daily regimen that will help keep your sales garden blooming:

- Make 10% more calls per day,
- Ask for the Sale 10% more often,
- Get up for work 10 minutes earlier each day. Spend this time on self-improvement, tending your garden of sales knowledge and skills,
- Give 10 sincere compliments to your prospects each week (2 compliments per day).

If you stick to this plan for two weeks, you will see some immediate short-term results, and there are many long-term rewards to harvest by maintaining this discipline.

Have You Written Down Your Goals?

You've heard it a million times, "Write down your goals." If you had a dime for every time someone said that, you wouldn't need to write them down, they'd be actualized!

So, why haven't you done it? It really does work. Dreaming about selling that national retailer and committing to the sale are two entirely different things. Some of the keys to setting and meeting goals are:

> *The finest eloquence is that which gets things done.*
> *—David Lloyd George*

1. **Make your goals specific.** If your goals aren't clear, how will you know when you've reached them? "I will sell the XYZ hotel chain."

2. **Make your goals attainable.** If you don't see a goal as reasonable, it's not a serious goal, it's a fantasy. "I will sell the XYZ hotel chain in three months."

3. **Use motivating language.** "In three months, I will succeed in proving to XYZ Hotel that my service is the best for the company and I will have a signed contract."

4. **Place your goals** where you will see them daily.

5. **Set mini-goals.** Write these mini-goals on your daily calendar. Use specific numbers and dates. Make certain your mini-goals lead to your ultimate goal. Breaking them down will motivate you as you head toward your ultimate goal. "I will call XYZ this Wednesday. I will find the decision-maker by Friday. I will speak with the decision-maker by Tuesday, the 14th. I will meet the decision maker by Friday the 24th."

6. **Prioritize your goals** so they make sense. If you know you need to cold-call before you can schedule a meeting, make certain the cold call goals are before the prospecting calls.

Natural talent, intelligence, a wonderful education, none of these guarantees success. Something else is needed: the sensitivity to understand what other people want and the willingness to give it to them.

—John Luther

7. **Monitor yourself.** If you don't achieve a goal, find out why and move on. Learn from your shortcomings, but don't dwell on them.

8. **Share your goals.** Involve your friends and family in your sales efforts. They'll motivate you to keep on track and celebrate with you when you succeed.

9. **Be positive.** Be sure to focus on your accomplishments and commend yourself for the goals you have achieved!

Self Motivation

In theory, it's pretty obvious that positive reinforcement goes a lot farther than negative criticism. But, when you're frustrated with a situation or performance, it's hard to refrain from faultfinding.

The same applies when you are assessing your own sales performance. When you are analyzing your sales skills, or just having an internal dialogue, be careful to avoid negative self-talk, such as, "Cutting down the competition was stupid. Now I've lost the account." Learn from your failures and focus on your achievements, "The comparisons between companies was good; next time I will make it a little less personal."

Although it may seem to defy logic, sometimes the most effective method of changing your sales performance is giving your motivation a shot in the arm with affirmations of your determination and your ability, along with a hefty dose of positive feedback. Try It!

What It Takes To Succeed

Compare your sales performance with athletic success rates. You may be a better hitter than you thought.

Ability To Deal With Failure

In Sports: Even the most successful hitters in baseball, with career batting averages in the .333 range, fail to hit the ball two out of every three times at bat.

> *It's what you learn after you know it all that counts.*
> *— John Wooden*

In Sales: Out of every 10 sales calls, you are likely to see only four people, to get an extended time for presenting your product or service two times, and to close a sale maybe once if you've done everything right and you have some luck. You have to be able to deal with failure.

High Self-Esteem

In Sports: No matter what's happening in the game, the highly successful athlete keeps on plugging because he or she knows that it's nothing personal. The breaks are bound to come again, and it's important to stick with what got you into the game.

In Sales: Selling slumps are legendary. Everyone has them. Top salespeople know how to get out of them— fast. They make more calls, refresh their selling skills, read motivational books, talk to other top producers— they get moving.

Self Discipline

In Sports: Discipline drives the successful athlete. Cal Ripkin is a perfect example of the greatest self-discipline an athlete can have. Although he is not a super performer, he makes up for it with a discipline that is cast in steel.

In Sales: No sales career takes off without applying the basics over and over, day after day. It's not enough to shine for one sale and then let yourself fall apart for a week. The daily discipline of making calls and callbacks, doing the homework, and following up on promises, creates a climate for sales success.

Eight Winning Sales Strategies

In many sales technique books authors will offer a list of approaches and strategies to becoming a better sales professional. Of course, I would be remiss if I did not close this section with at least some great reminders of the things you already know.

1. You can not consistently function in a manner inconsistent with the way you see yourself. If you are depressed and discouraged in your state of mind, then you will function in this way. If you find yourself down, then get yourself some motivational tapes, and get pumped up. If you think these tips are silly, think again. They work.

2. Sales are 7% what you say, 38% how you say it, and 55% how you look. This, of course, is why companies such as IBM have in the past imposed a rigid dress code. IBM employees were not to make a significant positive or negative statement with their attire, but rather, a neutral one. Make your product or service memorable, not your attire.

3. Always be prospecting, even when you do not get the sale. (Which, by the way, will be more often than not.) Get the information that you came for and perhaps a lead as well.

> *A salesman is one who sells goods that won't come back to customers who will.*
> *—Anonymous*

4. Be an expert and /or a specialist. If you sell BankCard services, know the lingo, and use it. Read the industry information so that you can be as knowledgeable as possible. Strength sells. Knowledge is power.

5. Have a positive attitude. Remember that you are a professional. Sales is not something that just anyone can do on the spur of the moment, any more than is brain surgery. It is a learned skill, and one that can be finely honed. Remember that the world turns on sales and sales is simply helping people make better decisions.

6. Be who you are and let people be who they are. A phony is easily spotted. We all know that you must believe in what you are selling. If you don't believe in what you are selling, then look for something else to sell. But also remember that all companies must pick an element of their market in which to excel. To be a really great company within an industry you do not have to be great at everything, but you must excel at one thing. For example, we know that Wal-Mart excels at low prices. You would not go to Wal-Mart

and be upset if you did not get superior service, because superior service is not what they are known for. Likewise, you would not expect low prices from Macy's. Consider that whatever product or service you sell, you must accept the strength or value statement of that product or service or find one that more closely fits you.

7. Try to remember that every "NO" puts you that much closer to a "YES." You must understand that this is part of the process (so what), and you must move on (next). This is why we say SWSWSWN. Some will, Some won't, So what, Next.

8. Make people you deal with feel very, very special. Remember, people decide to buy within the first seven seconds of a presentation. If you are an enthusiastic professional and treat your prospects with respect, they will give this back to you in kind. Today may not be the right "buying" time for them, but if you do your job correctly, the next time may be.

All eight strategies can be summed up in the three letters, RAP. They stand for **Rapport, Ask Needs,** and **Promote**. We are never too young or too old to learn how to RAP.

Cartoon by Bradford Veley, Marquette, MI

Chapter 4

Remembering the Basics

Remembering the Basics

Aren't you just sick and tired of some "know it all" telling you about sales basics? You know, the stuff that you have forgotten more about than **that** "expert" will *ever* know. Well, this is one more time, because even if you are dead sure that you already know it all, it's important to keep your skills razor sharp.

Sales fundamentals such as listening and needs analysis, may make the difference between closing and losing a sale, since we are in a business in which listening is very important, and where needs analysis never worked better. So here is a quick summary of the most important things a sales professional must master.

> *If you don't have a selling system of your own when you are face to face with a buyer, you will unknowingly default to his system.*
>
> *—David Sandler*

Listen intently. The 80/20 rule bears repeating: Spend 80 percent of your time listening, and only 20 percent talking. You're there to serve your customer's needs, but you won't be able to if you don't stop talking long enough to uncover them. Ask a lot of questions, and take notes on the answers to 1) force yourself to listen carefully and 2) help yourself remember important points of the conversation. Sit on the edge of your seat and be fascinated by what your prospect has to say. A big sale may be riding on his or her every word.

Ask questions first, present later. If your presentation doesn't highlight the features or benefits your prospects are interested in, it probably won't persuade them to buy. Make sure you understand their needs, wants, expectations, and feelings 100 percent so that your presentation hits all their hot buttons. Ask questions first to ensure that you don't share all your good news on page one; it may help build your prospects' trust by showing them that their needs come before your desire to sell to them.

Uncover needs, don't presume them. Just as no competent doctor prescribes a treatment before thoroughly examining a patient, you should let your prospects tell you what they need instead of assuming that you already know. Should you make a service recommendation without consulting them, they may question your competence and intentions. Remember, your prospects know themselves and their businesses best. Give them a chance to share that knowledge with you to benefit you both.

Talk to the decision-maker. Who wants to make a convincing presentation to an enthusiastic prospect with no purchasing power? Presentations demand a lot of work and time, so make sure you present only to those who can reward your effort with a sale. It may take longer to reach upper management, but trying to sell to anyone else simply wastes time—yours and theirs. Instead of presenting to the wrong people, spend your time data gathering at all levels of the organization and continue to work on getting to the right person.

Now that you have the short version, let's take it apart and look at the sales process, piece by piece.

Phone Tips

When calling prospects, you don't have to be Miss Manners, but it does pay to be courteous. Just a few simple actions can help ingratiate you to a prospect or screener and get you further in the conversation.

For example, if you are on a car phone, cell phone, or even an airphone, be sure to relay that information to the person on the other end of the line, and ask if he or she can hear you clearly. On that same note, avoid using a speakerphone if you are the only person making the call. Speakerphones can cut off the beginnings and endings of words (which makes phone numbers almost impossible to hear) and can make communication frustrating. It also makes the person you've called feel he or she is less important than whatever it is you're doing that is prohibiting you from holding the phone.

Finally, don't do business from home if you are going to have non-business noise and interruptions, such as children making noise in the background. Also, remember you placed the call, so don't accept other incoming calls or ask the person to wait while you talk to someone who has entered the room. Focusing all your attention on the call, and a little courtesy, can go a long way.

> *Men, like bullets, go farthest when they are smoothest.*
> —*Jean Paul Richter*

The Four Ws

As you know, selling involves a tremendous amount of information gathering. You already know **what** you're selling, but you still need to find out the **why, where, who,** and **when** of the sale.

Why

Identifying a reason for buying is imperative to a successful meeting. Knowing what motivates the prospect will help you position your service so that you make the sale. But how?

Use the answers to probing questions, such as the ones below, to help figure out **why** this merchant is in the market for your service and how you should tailor your presentation to meet those needs.

- ✍ What motivated you to meet with a representative from my company?
- ✍ You haven't used a (check or bankcard service) in the past, have you? What prompted you to shop for one today?
- ✍ How does my service fit in your business plan?
- ✍ What do you expect from this service?

Where

After you've taken the time to investigate why a merchant wants a service such as yours, now you need to find out **where** the decision power lies. In other words, is this person the decision-maker? To find out, try the following questions:

- ✍ Is the responsibility of this decision spread across several people?
- ✍ Will your supervisor have any input?
- ✍ How many people are involved in the decision to purchase?
- ✍ Who will sign the agreement?

> *In ambition, as in love, the successful can afford to be indulgent toward their rivals. The prize our own, it is graceful to recognize the merit that vainly aspired to it.*
> *—Christian Nestell Bovee*

Who

What about your competition? We all perform better if we know what we're up against. If you know which companies the prospect is considering, you can highlight the features and benefits you offer which the competition just can't. You can also anticipate objections, which will arise when comparing your company to another. Find out **who** your competition is by asking the following:

- ✍ What motivated you to meet with a rep from my company, rather than someone else's?
- ✍ What other solutions have you considered?
- ✍ From your point of view, do we have any competition?

When

Once you have the answers to these questions, you'll know: **why** the merchant is shopping for a service, **where** the decision power is, and **who** your competition really is. But you may still be uncertain if you should go for the close. If you go in too soon, the prospect may feel threatened and you'll lose the sale; too late, and the prospect may go somewhere else. The answers to the following will help you know **when** to go for the close:

- ✍ Are you planning to start right away or do you have a long-range plan?
- ✍ What steps does your company execute when going through a purchasing decision like this?
- ✍ When would you like your terminal programmed and ready for transactions?

Getting the answers to **why, where, who** and **when** will get you what you want: The Sale!

Effort

Why do some people seem "born to sell" while others flounder? Successful sales professionals know that success requires time, dedication, a thick skin, and a whole lot of **effort**.

Encourage your prospects to voice their buying concerns.

Find new perspectives and ways of approaching a situation.

Force yourself to work harder than others.

Overestimate the competition.

Realize your decision making power. Make a decision and if it doesn't work out, it doesn't work out! Learn from it and move on.

Take pride in your work.

As easy as some make it seem, successful sales professionals are those who work the smartest and the hardest.

Phone Hints for Less Stress

Some quick hints for your next phone appointment:

Before the meeting write down key points that you want to make. Even though they're ingrained in your brain and you're certain you will never forget them, write down a couple of words, such as "Increased Approvals," or "Lower Rates."

Write down common objection answers, such as "I understand you're busy. That's why we need to talk," or "Would you like a service that increases your sales without any added effort?" Again, you may think you will never forget them, but writing it down can't hurt.

> *Remember that the faith that moves mountains always carries a pick.*
>
> *—Anonymous*

Work on your communication skills. Record yourself on the phone and identify the points you need to work on. Make it a goal to read more trade publications.

Picture your prospect in your mind as you speak. This helps you to attach a person to the voice and see the prospect as someone with a common goal.

Schedule your phone calls wisely. If you are calling a restaurant, call between 3 and 5 p.m. For an auto dealership, after hours might be the best time to get past the phone screener.

Smile! A smile is perceptible over the phone and is infectious!

Put Out the RADAR

Sometimes when we're meeting with the company "Big Wig" we get caught up in the importance of the person and forget the basics of selling. If you start to get flustered or intimidated by the stature of the person, all you need to do is remember to put out your **RADAR.**

Respect everyone you come in contact with, from the person who answers the phone, to the parking attendant, to the receptionist, to the secretary, to the executive.

Ascertain the names of all the key employees and their assistants.

Do your homework on the industry. Find out about this particular company's goals and future plans and demonstrate that you understand their problems. Most importantly, make your service part of those plans and show you can solve those problems.

Avoid time wasters such as catch phrases or jokes to get the conversation started. Instead, ask for opinions on a current event in the industry

Refrain from using jargon or trying to sound like an expert in the industry by using big words and technical phrases.

Being prepared, staying focused, and maximizing your time will help you tune your RADAR to locate the perfect sale.

"It never fails. When I finally get around to asking a sales prospect for the order, I draw a complete blank on what I'm actually selling!"

Cartoon by Bradford Veley, Marquette, MI

Chapter 5

Call Preparation

Interviewing For Sales

Treat your sales calls like job interviews. You wouldn't go into a job interview without preparation, right? Put the same preparation into your sales call. View the account as a position that you're applying for, and as such, it requires that you persuade the personnel representative (prospect) that your product is the best applicant in the hiring pool.

First Step: What's your objective?

Before you arrive for a job interview, you know your objective. The obvious objective is to get the job, but on our résumés we are a little more delicate. We focus on how our objective will benefit our prospective employer. For example, résumés don't state the objective as, "To get a job to pay my bills." Instead they say, "To utilize and further enhance my selling skills." The sales call demands the same finesse. While your objective is to close the sale, that doesn't benefit your prospect. An objective that is focused on the prospect's needs, such as "To help you maximize your time, increase your sales, and reduce your risk" is more appropriate.

> *In preparing for battle I have always found that plans are useless, but that planning is essential*
> *—Dwight D. Eisenhower*

Second Step: Are you prepared?

Any job applicant worth his/her salt researches the company before the interview. Doing the same for a sales call shows the prospect you're interested in their business. It also helps you determine their needs.

Third Step: Will there be any surprises?

Before an interview, applicants can anticipate the standard interview questions and have thoughtful answers prepared. Do the same for your prospecting call. For example:

"Why should I hire you?" (Why should I purchase your product?) An interviewer is looking for someone who can do the job, and do it well. They want someone with experience and skills. The same applies to sales. You must be able to show how your product can meet the needs of the company and offer added benefits.

"What are your strengths?" (What does your product do well?) If an applicant doesn't know his/her strengths, how can he expect the hiring company to find him valuable? Knowing what your product does well and articulating this to the prospect is vital.

"What are your weaknesses?" (What don't people like about your service?) Applicants don't rattle off, "I'm picky and like to pawn my work off on others." Instead, take those attributes and turn them into positives, such as "I'm detail-oriented and like to work in groups." Do the same with your product. For example, if some people feel your terminal takes too long to print reports and has a large footprint, you might say, "Our terminal prints extremely detailed reports. Also, our keys are larger so your staff can see them better."

Fourth Step: Did you get the job?

If an applicant is offered the job, great! But what if a hiring decision isn't made that day? The smart applicant sends a follow-up thank you letter. Sales pros who do the same are telling their prospects that they are professionals who seriously want their business.

So, brush up on your interviewing skills. You may not need a new job, but you can always use new sales!

Don't Forget the Basics

As a sales professional, you know that in order to keep selling you have to stay on your toes. We sometimes tend to forget the simplest things, which may be the most important things to the potential buyer.

For example, most of us are lazy when it comes to research. For large accounts you need to have a basic profile of the company, such as the annual revenue and the names of the corporate officers, before you meet with them. For small accounts, you need to know how they will use your service or product.

For large accounts, it is also a good idea to target several people with varying levels of influence within the company. When speaking to them, mention conversations with the others that you have met or spoken with. This makes it difficult for any one of them to ignore you.

The will to succeed is important, but what's more important is the will to prepare.

—Bobby Knight

Make sure that you clarify exactly what you are selling. If your product has a highly competitive market, then identifying specifics gives you a distinct edge over the competition.

Put yourself in your prospect's shoes. Pay close attention to your manner and your body language. Are you lacking enthusiasm? Would you buy something from yourself? As I have said earlier in this book, you must believe in your product and be excited about it! And remember, if it doesn't ring true it's just another sales pitch.

Ask yourself a closing question. Will the prospect feel my commitment and enthusiasm for what I do as a professional? If not, why not?

Plan for Opportunity

Have you ever kicked yourself because you missed a great opportunity? Sure, we all have because, deep down, we know we didn't miss the opportunity because of someone else's actions or because we weren't in the right place at the right time. We missed it because we didn't recognize the opportunity or weren't prepared for it.

First, what is your definition of "opportunity"? Is it money falling from the sky? Is it someone walking up to you and asking to buy your service? These, my friend, are fantasies, not opportunities. Sure they could happen, but it's not likely. What is likely is that you will get the sales and earn more money if you know how to recognize opportunities and are prepared for them.

> *Occasions are rare; and those who know how to seize upon them are rarer.*
>
> *—Josh Billings*

Opportunities don't arise from being in the right place at the right time. Yes, sometimes there are fortuitous circumstances that nudge us toward an opportunity, but nothing can assure that you recognize and take advantage of an opportunity like the habit of preparing for it in advance.

You can't rely on luck. Luck doesn't really exist. Preparation does. Some people may say, "She's really lucky. Everything falls into place for her." Actually, what she probably is, is prepared. She planned for the good fortune, anticipated it, learned how to recognize it, and most importantly, planned what to do when it did happen.

Crystal CLEAR

What makes an achiever? Achievers have a vision of what they want to accomplish and how they will do it. They have a **CLEAR** image of how they will succeed.

Achievers are **Communicators.** Very few people become successful all by themselves. On their way to the top, they communicate their ideas, questions, and concerns to others.

Achievers are **Listeners.** They hone their listening skills to become attuned to others' needs. Once they're aware of others' concerns, they can incorporate those concerns into their plans.

Achievers are **Efficient** in their processes. You can be the smartest person in the world but if you can't accomplish goals or maximize resources, you won't be a success.

Achievers are **Able.** They generally can get the job done, but if they can't, they find someone who can.

Achievers are **Ready.** They are poised at all times to take advantage of an opportunity and make things happen.

If you want to be an Achiever, fine tune your communication and listening skills, increase efficiency by maximizing time and effort, take part in on-going education and training to better your abilities, and always be ready for the next opportunity. (I guess I have beat that point enough.)

Be Prepared, Be Very Prepared

After hundreds of sales calls, you may be tempted to approach each call with the attitude that "They're all the same," and thus, treat them all the same. But, each possible sale involves prospects, and prospects are people. As we all know, no two people are alike; therefore, no two prospecting opportunities are alike. You must prepare for each one individually. Each call must be specifically targeted to that person and that business.

Before you arrive at the meeting, know exactly how you will target your service to each prospect before you arrive at the meeting. What will you stress? What will you offer? How will you negotiate? If you sit down and figure out the answers to these questions before every meeting, you will realize that each selling situation is truly unique.

Shhhh!

We spend a lot of time on our presentations, rehearsing what we will say, practicing how to say it, forming the standard answers to the standard objections. How about this for a change, practice not saying anything!

> *Silence is the ultimate weapon of power.*
> *—Charles De Gaulle*

After you've had the opportunity to briefly outline your service, ask the merchant what he thinks so far, and then stop talking. Even if it gets a little awkward, just wait for the merchant to tell you his feelings about his business and your service. Don't settle for yes/no answers. Given the time, the prospect will talk.

This opportunity to be heard will be a welcome surprise to someone who is anticipating a salesperson to suffocate him with sales jargon and the hard sell. It will also prevent your answers and comments from sounding "canned." The merchant will feel that you actually care about him and his business, and you will find out what it is this specific merchant needs and how your service can get him there.

Cartoon by Bradford Veley, Marquette, MI

Are You Qualifying, or Wasting Time?

Did you know that if you wish to make $100K per year, each hour of your time is worth over $48.00? Can you really afford the time to go back, send a proposal, or to be too timid to ask for the sale?

No one wants to waste time. You do not want your time wasted, and prospects feel the same way. A Professional Salesperson will always qualify the person he or she talks to before giving a presentation to prevent wasting time or having to make yet another visit. Every sales professional must quickly learn to determine who is the decision-maker and qualified buyer within a prospect's business setting.

The person you talk to must have the authority to approve (sign the Service Agreement) and implement the service for their place of business. The following are examples of questions you may want to ask to discover who is the decision-maker, and who is not:

> *Waste neither time nor money, but make the best use of both. Without industry and frugality, nothing will do, and with them everything.*
>
> *—Benjamin Franklin*

☞ Would you make a decision on this service or would you need to consult with someone?

☞ Are all the headaches of running this store yours or do you have someone to share them with?

☞ Would you like someone to sit in with us or do you make the decision alone?

(OK, just once more.) Once you have determined that the person you are talking with is a qualified decision maker, you can give your sales presentation knowing at the very least, that you are not going to hear, "Well, I will have to talk to (blank) about this."

Chapter 6

Prospecting

Prospecting

Since your clients do not come to you, you have to go out and find them. Your first steps in identifying potential customers must be prospecting.

Your sales success depends largely on how well and how many ways you prospect. You must keep yourself well supplied with people to call. An artful mix of prospecting will make you successful. Your prospect must meet three basic qualifications.

1. The need for the service,
2. Authority to make decisions, and
3. Most importantly, the ability to sign a check and the service agreement.

Most salespeople don't enjoy prospecting so they don't invest much time in it. But look at the steps in the sales cycle below:

- ☞ Planning
- ☞ Prospecting
- ☞ Meeting
- ☞ Recommending
- ☞ Closing

> *Nothing is really work unless you would rather be doing something else.*
> *—James Matthew Barrie*

None could be accomplished without prospecting!

If you are successful at prospecting, you will be a successful salesperson. So, it pay$ off to increase the time you spend prospecting, and you don't have to increase it much. Top producers are the ones who make that one extra call when the others give up.

Most salespeople avoid prospecting due to a fear of rejection. The key to overcoming that fear is to alter your perception of prospecting. How? Focus on how prospecting has been the way to make money.

Prospecting should be welcomed, rather than feared, because it allows you to control your financial destiny. In fact, the size of your commission check is directly related to the number of calls you make. In other words, you determine your level of income.

Have you ever heard that selling is the same as farming? Well, not exactly the same but there are some similarities, such as long hours and seasonal fluctuations. **The biggest similarity is that both farmers and salespeople reap what they sow.** If you want an abundant harvest, you must sow many seeds.

Prospecting is a goal, and you should treat it like one. Allow yourself to feel elated when you schedule an appointment. Why? Because you have sold someone on the idea of spending valuable time with you. Take that elated feeling and use it to transfer enthusiasm about your service to the buyer.

Don't get discouraged. Remember, sales is a process, not an event, and you can't lose if you control when it ends. Make sure the selling process ends only after you've converted your prospect into a satisfied client.

Cold Calls

> *The mode by which the inevitable comes to pass is effort.*
> *—Oliver Wendell Holmes*

Cold Calls in person are a highly effective method of prospecting, although most sales representatives would rather not do them. There are several major advantages to unannounced visits to your prospect's business location. You are able to evaluate the prospect's business first hand, enabling you to tailor the presentation to his or her specific needs. Your best results are very often face-to-face.

Cold calling will prevent the ups and downs that cut into your income. Here are a few tried and true rules that, if followed, will help increase the number of presentations you give:

- Assume that the person is in charge, "Are you the owner?"

- Clerks and secretaries can be sold on letting you talk to the decision-maker if you sell them on the fact that what you wish to talk about is important.

- Try, "I have a situation and I wonder if you could help me?" Then ask "Who is the owner, president, etc., and is that person available?" This is a very effective way around screens.

- If you know the prospect's name, assume that you are expected, "Please tell Joe that Vic Right is here to see him." Be assertive. You must expect to get face-to-face. If you do not, you will not.

Once you get face-to-face:

- Question opener: "Would you like to increase your profits by 15% to 20%?"

- Benefit opener: "I have a service that can increase your profits."

- Story opener: People love a good story that relates to their type of business. If you have a story that solves a problem or helps increase business, your prospect will want to hear it. (Use the one on the first page.)

- Referral opener: "Mr. Johnson at Johnson's Hardware asked me to stop in and speak to you about..."

Direct Mail

> *Everyone lives by selling something.*
> —*Robert Louis Stevenson*

You may want to consider using a direct mail piece to generate sales leads for yourself. The use of direct mail has proven to be very successful in the payment service industry in general, and in the sale of bankcard and check services specifically. You should be able to close 50% of the merchants who respond to the mail piece. Check with your service providers, they often have wonderful pieces that you can use free of charge.

You should remember that the lowest price is not the only thing that the "Analytical" will pay attention to; however, you must quantify the results of things like "more sales, fewer declines, better service, faster equipment."

Cartoon by Bradford Veley, Marquette, MI

Telephone Prospecting

The person-to-person contact afforded by the telephone allows for interaction between you and the prospect, enabling you to qualify or reject them quickly.

☎ Identify yourself and your organization.

☎ Increase interest through remarks that establish your credibility as a problem solver.

☎ Mention a specific product or service and applications that can help your prospect.

☎ Sell an appointment.

☎ Confirm that you are speaking with a decision-maker.

Try these openings: "I've been assigned the responsibility of serving your account. I would like to take this opportunity to introduce myself and arrange an appointment to meet with you in person..." or

"I recently received your name from my corporation printout of key accounts and was interested in learning more about your company (firm, store, etc.)." or

"Are your presently using a ________ service?" or

"I expect to be in your area on Tuesday. Now, Mr. Prospect, I'd like to show you how my program will increase your profits. Is Tuesday good or would Wednesday be better?"

The pro is always supplied with prospects. Your success depends upon the skills you develop as a prospector. Remember, in-person cold calls have proven to be the most successful for the long term. Start looking for new prospects today, and if you never stop, neither will your income.

Fishing for Prospects

How often have you heard "I don't have enough good prospects to call?" Actually, this often indicates more of a lack of creativity on the part of the salesperson, than a true limitation on the marketplace.

Example: There was a salesperson with a very limited product. He sold locomotives. His only customer was Union Pacific Railroad. If anyone could have used this excuse, he could. But he didn't! He first found his way to small logging companies and eventually to Santa Fe Railroad.

While a lack of good prospects is possible, as the above example illustrates, it is generally not true.

The point is this: the business world today is a dynamic, teeming, world community of opportunities. The success or failure of a salesperson will normally rest on realizing that there are changes occurring constantly in the following areas:

> *Action to be effective must be directed to clearly conceived ends.*
>
> —*Jawaharlal Nehru*

✔ Personnel — A recent study involving hundreds of personnel departments showed that positions are changing at a rate of 50% every six months. Note this is positions, not necessarily people. The person you spoke to last year might have been promoted and replaced by someone more receptive to your views and/or product information.

✔ Situations — Changing policies or procedures may have made your product or service more viable to the prospect's new outlook. (Such as significant fraud losses during the Christmas season, building a need for check guarantee, or a change in bankcard or product & services. Over time, the products and services that you or your company offer will change (such as a price increase from Visa or MasterCard, or the availability of cellular point-of-sale terminals). Whatever the change may be, the wise salesperson will take advantage of these new opportunities in reviving "stale" prospects.

✔ You — Don't forget! You change with time and experience. Surely you are better at what you do than you were six months ago. Your product knowledge has increased as well. Don't let pride stand in your way, try those accounts that slipped through your fingers when you were new. You'll probably be amazed at how much better and stronger your "net" has become. Fishing for prospects is just like fishing for fish— it requires you to put a line, and sometimes a net, in the water.

Read All About It!

Do you read your daily newspaper? If you do, you probably read the front page, sports, and maybe, if you have time, the business section. But, do you actively read the paper with your residual or commission check in mind? Try reading the paper as a business assignment.

* Read the new business announcements. What better place to find new prospects?

* Read the classifieds. Check to see who is hiring new management and watch for merchants who've declined you previously. Once the new manager is settled, you'll have a fresh slate with the new person.

* Read the ads. Check to see who is having sales and when. If you can greet the merchant and talk about the big "Midnight Madness Sale" she just had, you'll show that you're truly interested in her business.

So read all about it! You may find that your leads are right there, in black and white.

Mingle Madness

> *For they conquer who believe they can.*
> *—John Dryden*

Mike always had the feeling whenever he was at a social gathering that everybody knew everybody else, and that he was the only "outcast." At one business gathering, he decided to eavesdrop on a few conversations. He realized that most people were either struggling to make conversation with strangers, or they were standing through the entire event talking to the people they came with.

While you may be just fine when you are talking to a prospect one-on-one, many people, even those who have been in the sales profession for many years, find crowds a bit more difficult.

Mingling successfully basically means harnessing your confidence. Overcoming shyness gets easier once you have a few successes and promising experiences under your belt.

Mingling successfully also means that you must realize that "mingling" or "networking," as some say, can be very beneficial to your sales. Group presentation opportunities, from Chambers of Commerce to Rotary Club meetings, can give you access to the community in which you live. If you give these opportunities half a chance, you'll soon realize that you are probably more ahead of the game than many other people. After all, you are a "sales executive."

Even if you've had a bad experience, that shouldn't deter you from going out to mingle some more. Your prospect was probably suffering from a more acute case of anxiety or insecurity than you were.

It may help to ask an associate to accompany you to a future event. The important thing is not to rely on people you know for security to the extent that you don't venture out and meet new people on your own. Choose someone you are comfortable around who understands your shyness, and who will introduce you to a few contacts they'll no doubt meet during the event.

When you do strike up a conversation, listen actively and be genuinely interested in what your speaker has to say. Take notes if it's appropriate, so that you can follow up.

The contact is just a starting point, and can be a major source of business for you.

Networking

If you're attending a conference or seminar, or simply having lunch with some colleagues, how do you identify the people who **can** help you and are willing to do so?

Before the Event

Before you attend a seminar or other business gathering, do some detective work. View this as a prospecting opportunity for networking and treat it as you would treat a prospecting opportunity for sales. Find out all you can about the people who will be there. Ask around your associates, go online and do a simple search under proper names or companies, or visit local papers (either online or in person) and see if any of the attendees have been in the news and why.

During the Event

Once you meet a potentially valuable contact, make a commitment. Listen intently and invest your time and energy in your time together. Even if you think you may be at a dead-end and neither of you can help each other, give it some time. You may learn that this person really can help you reach your goals.

> *Opportunity is missed by most people because it is dressed in overalls and looks like work.*
>
> *—Thomas Alva Edison*

OK, so you've chatted with your new contact. Now's the time to commit all the important data to memory. Don't limit the data to what they do and whom they work for—you have a business card for that. Note other items, such as a bit about their history, or a new endeavor they're excited about. Find ways in which your interests merge or complement each other.

As you get to know your new contact, remember that networking isn't just about what the contact can do for you; you can be a very valuable and interesting contact for him or her. Sure, you wake up as the same person every day, and you do the same job every day. You may even be getting a little bored with yourself. But, your contact is meeting you for the first time. You are an ambassador for your industry, your company, and yourself. Don't play down what you do or the importance of your position. Make it exciting.

Here's the important part: What is your link to each other? What can you do to help your new contact? What can you do now that will further both of your careers? If you don't know the answers to these questions, ask! A simple, "What projects are you working on now? Do you think I might know someone who could help you with that?" Questions like this can get you the answers you need. Extending a helping hand could make all the difference both now and down the road when you need a hand.

Brainstorming for Success

> *The vitality of thought is in adventure. Ideas won't keep. Something must be done about them. When the idea is new, its custodians have fervor and live for it.*
> *—Alfred North Whitehead*

One way to stimulate growth and profits is to break away from your normal routine and find new sources for leads. If you usually depend on cold calls or a "leads group," look around for other opportunities. How long has it been since you checked the business directory or the phone book? What about checking magazines and television ads? Friends and neighbors are often another good source (it's who you know, remember). Set a goal of one new prospect every time you visit the mall or supermarket. When it's time to get your sales piece in front of the customer, use an innovative approach. Add punch to your introductory letter by enclosing a small gift they will remember. Finally, make your presentation memorable by using humor tailored to your new prospect's business.

Another key to success is to brainstorm about potential obstacles in your industry and have a plan of action ready. How will technology affect your industry in the next six months? How will it influence your customers' purchasing decisions? Stay abreast of potential changes and formulate plans ahead of time. Often, being the first one with a solution means getting the account.

Stimulate sales by jump starting your creative thinking process. Think of new and different ways to solve old problems without worrying about how practical they are for the moment. Write them down, no matter how silly they may seem. Later, expand each idea into several more. When this process is complete, you can switch to practical thinking to edit and reformulate the list. Also, avoid negative thinking patterns by playing the "what if" game. Allow your mind to indulge a little in the answers that emerge. You may discover some new strategies for dealing with challenges you face every day. Share your discoveries with your co-workers. New ideas are often springboards to creativity.

Break from routine and take the time to brainstorm and think outside of the box. It may be just what you need to jump-start your sales.

Valid Prospect or Information Gatherer?

You're pitching a business owner and you've presented all the benefits, but you still can't judge whether this person is on a scouting mission or is really a valid prospect.

Try asking some probing questions, like the ones below, to help ferret out the truly interested from the looky-lou:

▼ What are you looking for in a ______ provider?

- What is your idea of a good ______ service? A great service?
- How do you see ______ changing your business?
- How many employees will be using the service directly? Are you planning a training session?
- What will influence your buying decision most: price, flexibility, or convenience?

Whether you determine the merchant to be a valid prospect or merely someone who is curious, don't miss this opportunity to promote your service. Even a person who is not interested may know someone who is, or may become a valid prospect down the road. However it turns out, you can never get too much practice.

Rooting for Referrals?

So you have run out of reference ideas. Try this: sit down and make a list of everyone you know. Include everyone from the guy you see at the gas station to that high school friend you run into now and again. But, most importantly, be sure to include those who've sold you something, such as your realtor, landlord, insurance agent, and auto mechanic.

After you have your list, make it a point to ask two people a day for referrals. Give them your card to pass on to others who could use your service. This takes the pressure off your acquaintances while giving you an opportunity to increase your contact list. Some of the most successful ISOs have built their businesses out of referrals. You just need to force yourself to give it a try. It works!

Voice Mail

Voice mail is one of those technological advances people either love or hate. There are actually still people out there who won't leave messages because they can't stand to hear themselves on tape!

> *Every improvement in communication makes the bore more terrible.*
> —*Frank Moore Colby*

Whether you can't bring yourself to leave messages or whether you consider voice mail an essential tool, it is a fact of business life. Remember, voice mail messages are worth nothing until they are returned. To get the most out of your voice mail messages, follow these tips:

- Sound excited
- Keep your message under 30 seconds
- Smile when speaking
- Speak slowly and clearly
- Repeat your name, phone number, and company
- Spell your name and company name
- Don't give away ALL your information, just enough to make the person want to call you back!

It may be helpful to practice your message on your own voice mail and then listen to it yourself to identity the areas you need to work on.

With a little practice, you'll have the message that gets returned.

What if They Call Back?

Here are some tips to remember when customers or even prospects call while you're out:

1. The caller can always call a competitor who is in. So return the call ASAP, by the end of business the next day, at the very latest.

2. Never let an answering service or employee ask the prospect to call back. Train your staff to get the name, company, number, and reason for the call. (If you have voice mail, ask for those specific items). Then put the responsibility to call back on you.

3. Even if you have the cheapest and/or best service on the planet, it will not make up for inaccessibility. In this day of cell phones, pagers, and all manner of electronic communications, you have to be as accessible as possible.

> *Each mind is pressed, and open every ear, to hear new tidings, though they no way joy us.*
>
> *—Edward Fairfax*

4. Your callers shouldn't have to try to maneuver through a confusing voice mail system, they may call someone else if your system is too difficult.

5. Always sound delighted that the person chose to call you. Instruct your staff to do the same. The caller doesn't have to tolerate indifference—from you or your staff. They could've just as easily chosen to call someone else (and they still can!).

6. Provide a time when you will be able to return calls. If you have a receptionist or other communications assistants, let them know when you will be returning calls. Set aside a specific block of time to return calls each day.

The caller's impression of your business is vital, even when it is of your phone system.

Direct Mail

Direct marketing has become a very popular way to sell services and products. If your company uses direct marketing, you may be able to increase its effectiveness by considering the following tips.

1. Keep the package simple. Use concise copy and a simple design. Lengthy copy may include information that discourages the prospect from responding. A busy layout may cause the reader to focus on the design, not the service you are trying to sell.

2. Make strong offers and state them up front. Let the prospect know how he or she will benefit from this offer. State the offer boldly so the reader can't miss it.

3. Use colors and a design that motivate the reader to act. Bold colors, such as red, green, and blue, will attract attention. Avoid pastel, muted colors and soft designs that pacify the reader.

4. Don't try to accomplish too much with your marketing piece. Too many objectives will distract the reader. You will enjoy a higher response rate if you concentrate on just one goal.

5. Write copy that motivates your readers to act. Sell the idea of success and a better future. Use positive words, such as free, value, and save, that instill confidence in your product. Avoid negative words such as cost and pay.

6. Don't try to appeal to everyone. Your package will lose its focus and then you will appeal to no one.

How Do You Deal with Apathy?

> *Apathy is a sort of living oblivion.*
> *—Horace Greeley*

How do you convince a prospect to make time for you and your presentation? We've all had the experience of calling on a prospective customer who really doesn't care about our services and sees no need to talk to us. How do you get your foot in the door?

Well, first figure out why that person doesn't want to talk to you. Is it because of apathy, or is it something else? Does this person actually have an opinion of your service, negative or positive? If the answer to the latter question is "yes," then apathy is not your problem. If the prospect has taken the time to form an opinion, it means there is room for you to prove yourself and change his/her mind.

If the merchant is disinterested, find out why. Do you believe your service is really going to benefit this person's business? (It will be pretty difficult to convince someone that they need your service if you don't believe it yourself.)

Finally, make yourself stand out from the hundreds of others sales professionals (and not so professionals) that a merchant sees daily. Ask yourself, "How can I make this merchant's job easier? How can I make daily activities more profitable?" Then show the merchant how.

Slow Business Season Can Mean Good Selling Season

Every business has lulls. They may be the result of seasonal fluctuations or serious depressions. Whatever the reason for a drop in sales, it's an excellent opportunity for you. You'll probably encounter less competition and less interruption. So, when you hear, "Business is slow," use the following responses to increase your sales and the merchant's.

> *I am the worst salesman: therefore, I must make it easy for people to buy.*
> *—Frank W. Woolworth*

1. I'm glad I'm here! We can start fixing that right now!

2. I'm sure you're planning to change that. Perhaps my service fits into that plan.

3. With this temporary lull, isn't this the perfect time for us to discuss this opportunity with minimal interruption?

4. I've met with a lot of merchants in the same situation and fortunately, we were able to work together to fix the situation.

5. I have a list of merchants who use the service and their sales have increased as a result. Would you like to see it?

6. So you're cutting back on purchases? What are your priorities? If increasing sales or minimizing risk is one, then this is one area you won't want to cut back on.

7. I'm sure you don't anticipate business to remain slow. You want to be prepared for the rush when business picks up. I can help so you aren't caught with your guard down.

The seemingly bad news of a merchant's decreased sales can actually be good news for you. The increased availability will make the merchant more receptive to your proposition and result in good news for both of you. In addition, remember your competitors may actually believe the slow season myth and stay home, leaving the door open for you.

Chapter 7

The Sales Call

Motivating Change

Human beings are all naturally resistant to change. But, as selling professionals, it is our job to motivate others to change: Change their thinking, change their habits.

How can we make change less scary for our prospects? How can we encourage them to leave the safe familiarity of their old ways of doing things and sign with our service or use our equipment?

Demystify

For many people, resistance to change stems from a fear of the unknown. They are wondering:

> *The best way to get on in the world is to make people believe it's to their advantage to help you.*
> *—Jean de La Bruyere*

- ☞ What exactly will happen if I switch to a new terminal?
- ☞ What will this new service do for me?
- ☞ Will my customers see a difference?
- ☞ What benefits will I see?
- ☞ Is there anyone in my area who is using the same piece of equipment or service?
- ☞ What kind of training will I have to invest in?
- ☞ Do I have to learn new keystrokes?
- ☞ Do I have to buy new supplies?

It is your job to answer all these questions, even if they're never verbalized. Many prospects have questions running through their heads that they never ask. Use specifics, cite details, ask questions. Make sure nothing goes unanswered.

Clarify

Remember that the service or equipment the prospect is purchasing is new to him or her-no matter how detailed your presentation. And the more versatile the product, the more intimidating the thought of being left alone with it! The possibilities of your product or service build hope, but to build confidence, you must get down to the basics. After you have demystified your product, go back and clarify the following:

- ✗ Exactly what this terminal does.
- ✗ Exactly how it will be set up.
- ✗ Exactly when they will be up and ready.
- ✗ Exactly how the customer interfaces will be affected.
- ✗ Exactly what benefits they will see (quieter printer, wireless capability, etc.).
- ✗ What keystrokes do what.
- ✗ What kind of upgrades are available/needed.
- ✗ What kind of security is available on the terminal.
- ✗ What kind of paper is used.
- ✗ What customizable features are available.

And don't forget to have your prospect do some clarifying, too. Ask again exactly what the merchant needs and wants. You can't meet those needs if you aren't certain what they are.

Compare

Finally, once you've taken the unknowns out of the buying decision, compare your prospect's current situation to the one they could enjoy if they signed an agreement with you. Once they have the whole picture, they will see that you can offer them a better product — if only they'll make a change.

Getting Past the Awkward Moments

Sometimes the first meeting with a prospect can be awkward. After the business cards are exchanged, what do you say next? You've never seen this person before, and it seems a little rushed to start the presentation immediately. It may help to take a few minutes and get to know the person a bit before jumping in with both feet. Try the following transition phrases to start building a relationship with the prospect.

> *The meek shall inherit the world, but they'll never increase market share.*
> *— William G. McGowan*

1. Your staff is very personable. Do you have special employee programs to keep moral up?
2. I saw you in the paper (saw your company on the business page, etc.), do you have a PR department or do you do that on your own?
3. I saw an article about your type of business in Sunday's paper. Did you see it?
4. This is an excellent location. Do you get a lot of traffic from XY store?
5. It seems that you run the show around here. How many hours per week are you here?
6. I see your plaque on the wall. Who is it from?

Given the opportunity, most prospects will tell you more than a little about themselves. Armed with this knowledge, you will have a better chance of breaking the ice and leaving a favorable impression on the prospect, and a signed service agreement too!

I'm Not Interested

If you have heard it once, you have heard it a thousand times: "I'm not interested!" If this is not your experience, you should ask yourself if you are spending enough time on the street. Indeed, the response most often given by a prospect is that they are happy doing nothing. Of course, your job is to make them want to do what human nature compels them not to do: Do something! Make a change!

What do you do when you hear, "Thanks anyway, but our current service is fine." Do you walk away? Of course not!

But, the merchant has a point, if they're satisfied with their current service, why should they change to yours? Because your service will WOW them, rather than just meet their basic needs. Try the following responses to show them what they're missing!

> *No gain is so certain as that which proceeds from the economical use of what you already have.*
>
> *—Latin Proverb*

"Great, I like to deal with merchants who make good decisions. But, when the decision was made to go with company X, maybe you didn't know about us. That may have been the best choice then, but now we offer..."

"You may feel you're satisfied because you weren't aware of all we offer. Let me tell you some of our benefits and you'll see how you can go from satisfied to ecstatic."

"Did you have a different company before your current one? Why did you change? Were you happy that you did? Well, it can be even better!"

"I think I understand what you're saying. You don't want to go through the effort of changing. Well, I can give you a variety of reasons why this change will be good for you, your business, and your personal well being. You won't waste business time and resources chasing payments and you'll have more time for a personal life."

"What do you like best about your current service? Well, let me tell you how we can expand on that and give you the best possible service."

"OK, but as you know, business is tough and there is always someone nipping at your heels. To thrive and not just survive, your service has to be exemplary. We know that, and that's why we strive to provide the best (not just adequate) service. We want you to be thrilled with your service, not just satisfied."

"Of course you're satisfied, and the service is fine. But, don't you want more than just the status quo? Don't you want something better for your business?"

"Is it really fine? How many claims did you submit last month? Did you have to call customer service? Why? Did you get a prompt response? Was it the response you wanted or was it just "fine".

There are many companies whose service is fine. The key is showing your prospect that your service is exceptional.

Word Choice

You wouldn't open a meeting with, "You're not interested in my product, are you?" Of course not. It's absurd to set yourself up for rejection like that. But sometimes we inadvertently set ourselves up for a "No." It may not be as obvious as the example above, but it is certainly as deadly.

Look at the following examples to find better ways to phrase your introductions so they are the beginnings of beneficial meetings rather than excuses for your prospect to dismiss you.

Average: "Do you have a moment or should I come back later?"
Better: "Let's spend a brief moment outlining my service."

Average: "Do you have a check problem?"
Better: "Let's discuss how we can make checks a safer form of payment."

> *Words are tools which automatically carve concepts out of experience.*
> *—Julian Sorrell Huxley*

Average: "Do you want to hear about my service?"
Better: "This is what my service does better than what you have now: ..."

Average: "What would you say if I told you I could increase your sales"
Better: "Here are some ways I can increase your bottom line: ..."

Opening communication is vital to your presentation but so is maintaining control. If you structure your statements carefully, you will allow your prospects to contribute to the conversation and offer helpful data without giving them the opportunity to stop negotiations before they start.

As you read this, you may be thinking, "I've read this before in a variety of sales literature." Well, you probably have, and there's a good reason.

We are all guilty of hanging on to the same old terms and phrases and using them over and over. (You know the culprits: save, cost, profits, few minutes of your time, money.) The only way to break the habit and add some life to your language is to constantly access new ideas and continually examine the problem to be sure you're not falling back into the same old patterns.

Instead of using tired words that have lost their pizzazz, try some other words with action. For example:

> Rather than asking for "A few minutes of your time," use words which stress that this is a venture the two of you are embarking on together. Instead of asking for time to present to the merchant, ask for some time to discuss and analyze the merchant's business strategy.
>
> In the place of "save," try slash, shrink, slice, trim, modify, eliminate, or salvage.
>
> Instead of "cost," how about expense, charge, waste, or burden?
>
> Rather than "profits," insert dollars, revenue, cash, income, or market share.

Finally, take a break from phrases such as, "With our service you can..." or "Our service will let you..." try substituting maximization verbs such as strengthen, intensify, boost, or build. For example, "With our custom program you will boost your sales and enhance your market share."

Inserting fresh action words in the place of tired ones is especially effective if you repeat what the prospect said and replace their hackneyed word or phrase with your new, invigorating phrase.

Sales Presentation Tips

As you move up the prospective account food chain, it becomes more and more important to "know your prospect." This can vary from simple information gathered from other employees of the prospective account, to being able to use the prospect's own jargon.

A great salesperson speaks to accounts in their own language. Your object isn't to make prospects think you know as much about their business as they do, but rather to make them feel that you understand their problems, their viewpoints, and their needs.

Using your prospects' lingo is the most efficient way to establish rapport with many different groups of people. We identify with people who share things with us. We instinctively feel less fear and more trust in them. For this very reason, many successful salespeople target a type of business to concentrate their sales efforts on, so they catch onto the lingo.

Examples:

- ☞ When talking to the controller of an auto dealership, you would refer to the position responsible for securing financing for consumers and completing the paperwork for the sale as the "F&I person."

- ☞ When talking to the controller of a hotel, you would call the detail of the hotel charges "the folio."

How do you learn this lingo? Read trade magazines and make notes of any new words and viewpoints. Pay close attention to the editorials and letters to the editors. They will provide you with authentic viewpoints of people involved with that special interest.

Prior to contacting the prospect, you must first plan your presentation. One of the most important things you can do is research your prospect. Published directories will give you an enormous amount of information. Such directories are found in the business section of your public library.

Check out *Who's Who, Standard & Poor's Directory,* and *Dun & Bradstreet Million-Dollar Directory* for starters. When you arrive at the store, talk to the sales clerks and managers to obtain additional information.

Once you have researched your prospect, use the information you gained and apply it towards defining their needs. Carefully uncover their negative feelings. Never work yourself into a situation where you're knocking their current process or service provider, because that's knocking their judgment. There's no faster way to chill your chances than to let your prospect know you think he or she has previously made a bad decision.

Example:

☞ Ask them what they would like to see improved or changed in their check program. Build your presentation around the things the prospects would like to see improved.

☞ Zero in on the Programs: Give them three choices. What is most important to you: cost, complete coverage, or lowest decline rate in the industry?

Focus on their choice. Frequently salespeople tend to focus on the features their service offers. A customer wants to know the benefit associated with the feature you offer. Remember, benefits sell your customer, not features, and talking the talk will help to create the trust and rapport to make the benefits shine.

Relax and Let the Magic Flow

As you know, merchants must be given the time to voice their opinions, to tell you their objections (so you can resolve them), and to work through their buying decision.

Are you still out of breath at the end of your presentation, and the merchant hasn't had a chance to get a word in edgewise? Try these tips to help you close your mouth and open the door to a sale:

> *Selling is like riding a bicycle—either you keep moving or you fall down.*
> *—Anonymous*

Relax—You may be nervous and afraid of "the pause." Therefore, you continue to talk to avoid the awkward silence. Don't be. Let the silence sit there so both you and the prospect can process what was said. Give the merchant an opportunity to respond.

Speak Slowly—Again, you may be nervous (or just excited), and have a tendency to speak quickly. Make a conscious effort to slow your speech and speak clearly and precisely. If you run through the presentation at lightning speed, the merchant may miss some of your most important points!

Choose Words Carefully—We've all had the experience of speaking with someone who talks a lot but doesn't really say anything. Think about what you say before you say it. Is it necessary? Will it help with the buying decision or the relationship you're trying to nurture?

Get To The Point—Do you use phrases such as, "In my opinion, it's been my experience," "Simultaneously, at the same time"? Avoid redundancy and stay with the facts. Filling your speech with unnecessary words wastes your prospects' time and may insult them should they feel you are being redundant because you think they're unable to understand you.

After a little practice, you'll be comfortable with silent pauses and ready to make some noise about your closed sales!

Typecasting

We've all heard that we should tailor our presentations to fit our prospects, using tools such as mirroring body language and using familiar phrases to put the prospect at ease and increase the likelihood of a sale. But, how do you know how to present yourself if you are meeting this person for the first time? Well, upon introduction, take a few minutes to size up the merchant and figure our what makes him tick. Then you can gear your presentation to be the most effective for that "type" of person.

> *People do not seem to realize that their opinion of the world is also a confession of character.*
> *—Ralph Waldo Emerson*

Some of the most common "types" of people you will encounter are: The Coordinator, The Manager, and The Associate.

The Coordinator—At first glance, a Coordinator may appear to be a Manager, but, upon closer examination you will recognize a Coordinator because they are charismatic and generally well liked. They prefer to be active, rather than sitting behind a desk, and enjoy the thrill of the chase. Lucky for you, Coordinators are usually drawn to calculated risks, so position your service as a well thought out risk, such as "gotta spend money to make money."

The Manager—Similar to the Coordinator, the Manager is a take charge person, but unlike the Coordinator, Managers may put some people off because they can be controlling and obsessive. They like to feel in control; therefore, don't pressure Managers into a decision. They may become defensive. You will need to be flexible and make Managers feel that they are controlling the meeting. A key is to focus on how your service will help them stay in control.

The Associate—Unlike the Manager and Coordinator, Associates tend to focus on the company as a whole and are usually trusted by co-workers. When calling on an Associate, you may find that he is polite and sensitive to your feelings, but that doesn't mean you have an easy sale. Associates need to feel that you are considering the feelings of the individuals in the company and that your service will help everyone. Of course, since the Associate focuses on the needs of others, he or she will need to consult others before making a buying decision. Be patient and you will have a better chance of getting the sale.

Knowing who your audience is can be the difference between a sale and a missed opportunity.

A Tough Call Made Easier

How do you deal with a merchant who has all the answers and just knows your service won't work for her?

Well, if you've been in this position before, you know that disagreeing doesn't get you anywhere. The merchant will just "stick to her guns" and/or become defensive.

Try this. Instead of saying something such as, "Well, I disagree, Ms. Merchant. Selectively accepting checks doesn't solve your check problems," try asking questions, such as, "How is selectively accepting checks working for you? Have you ever had to turn down a check you were uncertain of? How did you handle that situation? Did you convert that sale to another payment type, or did you lose the sale?" This can lead to a real conversation about the multiple payment options you offer, such as Multiple Check.

In addition, you've eliminated a possible stand off and given the merchant a chance to talk. It also opens up an avenue for the merchant to come over to your side, without embarrassment.

Also, as the merchant talks through her answer, she may allow some information that will help you with your presentation. She may even realize that you have some valid points, take some of your ideas, and incorporate them into her answer, thinking what you said is her idea. Of course, when this happens, you just know you have the sale.

Naming Names

Remembering and using your customers' and prospects' names lets them know how important they are. Here are some tips to help you improve this valuable sales skill and eliminate the excuse, "I'm no good with names."

> *Listening, not imitation, may be the sincerest form of flattery*
> *—Dr. Joyce Brothers*

Stay focused during introductions—don't let your attention wander when you are being introduced. Make direct eye contact with the person you're meeting and treat them as though they are the most important person in the room. They might be!

Listen carefully to the name and repeat it immediately—verbal repetition will reinforce the new name, allow you to rehearse it, and give you a simple way to clarify difficult pronunciations.

Create a correspondence—thinking of a favorite friend, relative, or famous personality with the same name will give you a memory jogger.

Use the name throughout your conversation—"Paul, just how do you decide which checks to accept?" Using the prospect's name builds rapport and strengthens your memory.

These tips will help you remember a new acquaintance's name, but if you forget or don't hear it the first time, ask for it! Asking for a person's name is much less embarrassing than using the wrong one. If the name is particularly difficult, ask the person to spell it.

Your prospects are your keys to the future. Focus, listen, associate, and use their names—they'll unlock the door to your success.

Persuade and Prosper

Here are four techniques for transforming prospects into willing customers.

1. "Please," "thank you," and your prospect's first name are among the most powerful words in your selling vocabulary. Another word that induces action is "because." Telling your prospects why they should buy will significantly increase your persuasive power.

2. Hypnotherapy research has shown that telling someone not to do something often has the reverse effect (any parent will vouch for this). Words like "might," "maybe," and "don't" can work in your favor. "Don't feel as though you need to sign now," or "Maybe you'll want to start tomorrow," give subliminal commands to buy that don't put your prospects on the defensive.

3. "What is the most important element in your decision regarding your financial services?" This question will help you uncover your prospect's values and allow you to custom tailor your presentation to meet his/her needs. Using questions to uncover objections will have your prospects telling you how to persuade them to buy.

4. If your product or service sounds too good to be true, your prospect might decide it is. By presenting one or two drawbacks to your service, you allow Mr. or Ms. Merchant to focus on the positives instead of trying to uncover what you're not telling him. "This system does require you to train all of your sales personnel; however, this investment does pay for itself as soon as you submit your........"

Targeting the Personality of the Decision Maker

If you've been pounding the pavement for any time at all, you know that there are different types of buyers out there.

In fact, these buying types are just as often found today in small- and medium-sized companies as they once were in large corporations.

Each time you make your pitch you need to tailor it to the personality of your prospect. This will allow you to answer their objections and lead them to the correct decision ... a buying decision.

Here are some personality types that you will meet along the road to your next pinnacle of success. None of these types are limited to a specific gender, and some examples may be exaggerated (you be the judge).

Priscilla Purchaser—Punctilious Priscilla should have been an English teacher, but she's landed the purchasing position for a mid-sized retailer. She has a significant job and a parade of sales people travel through her office daily. Her decisions are based on price and performance, and she'll replace you with the competition at a moment's notice.

> *Only a fool holds out for the top dollar.*
> *— Joseph P. Kennedy*

Your presentation should be facts and figures. Don't try to smooth-talk this one, stick to your service's strengths and cost-saving benefits. You'll stand out from the crowd of "typical" salespersons maintaining a low profile. Remember your sales etiquette, confirm all of your meetings in writing and send thank you notes.

Bob Bargainer—Bob's role model is "Let's Make a Deal." He wants door number one and number two, and throw in the surprise gift while you're at it. However, if you give him anything he'll make sure that everyone knows about it (and possibly upset some of your customers/prospects along the way).

Bob is the type to ask you for a kickback for the "Association." Let Bob know that you may well be able to accomplish what he is asking. However, the Association Members must of course know that the Association will enjoy a piece of the members' discount rate. This will often eliminate the request, and at the very least, show Bob that you and your organization are honest. In all your dealings, let Bob know that you respect his business sense. You may not have to give the store away; try sending him "thank you" notes and a few extra phone calls. Point out which features' make the most sense in his business and how your service can positively affect his bottom-line. Honesty in dealings will often overcome, "Let's make a deal."

Marketing Moses—This guy knows exactly what he wants and wants it delivered on a silver platter. He will dot all the "i's" and cross all the "t's" and wants to control every aspect of the deal. Remain calm and superbly organized when dealing with Moses.

Confirm every detail, agreement, meeting, in writing. Fax your follow-ups, then mail the originals to him. Double check every figure you quote—don't let any disorganization enter into this relationship. Once Moses knows he can depend on you and your company, he'll remain committed to you.

Loyal Larry—Larry already thinks that the company you represent is the greatest. He may have become aware of the company from a friend or business associate. But you've just met, so show him your integrity through your excellent product knowledge and willingness to meet his special needs. Don't under-sell Larry. Provide the service he needs by keeping him abreast of product upgrades and new services.

Matching your presentation style to the prospect's personality will greatly enhance your closing percentage and allow you to appeal to a larger market. Your tone, pace, emphasis, and level of detail should be easily modified while you size up the merchant (say in the first 5 to 7 seconds of the meeting). Do your homework, and know your products and services so intimately that your professionalism is never in question. Remain positive, and remember, get the check.

Five Benefits of Silence in Sales

One of the best ways to learn about your prospect or customer is to use "Golden Silence". This is nothing more than using a pause at two points in your questioning: after you've asked the question, and after the listener has answered. Not just a brief pause, but a 2 to 3 second pause. Here are five of the benefits of this technique.

> *If you keep your mouth shut you will never put your foot in it.*
> *—Austin O'Malley*

1. You won't feel compelled to continue talking after asking the question if you force yourself to pause. People don't always immediately answer, and pausing gives them the opportunity to think a bit. Often, if you keep talking, you will give up something that you don't really need to say or do.

2. The number and length of responses will increase. People feel more comfortable when you give them time to frame their answers, which will likely be more comprehensive.

3. The amount of unsolicited information will increase. If you don't jump in immediately after they've answered, prospects are given a little more time to contemplate what they've just said. This may prompt

additional comments. Since information is power, having the objections to "the sale" voiced may permit you to address them early in the presentation.

4. You'll have more time to understand what they've said. Since you know you're going to pause, you can spend all of your listening time focused on the message, not on what you will say next.

5. You will have more time to formulate your next comment. After the prospect or customer has finished their answer, pause again. You can use your pause time to develop your next question or statement. You'll possess more relevant information because you have previously taken the time to listen, and given the time to answer.

"On the contrary, Hank, I believe that if you know precisely where a problem is, slapping a band-aid on it can be a VERY effective solution!"

Cartoon by Bradford Veley, Marquette, MI

Chapter 8

The Presentation

Improve Your Presentations

You're familiar with *Seven Habits of Highly Effective People.* Now we have Eight Ways to Improve Your Sales Presentations:

1. Look your prospect in the eye.
2. Use your prospect's name just two or three times during the presentation.
3. Avoid the passive voice.
4. Open up the floor to comments.
5. Listen actively, but don't interrupt.
6. Use "we" instead of "I".
7. Use "try," "could," or "may," in place of "need," "have to," or "must."
8. Smile!

> *Agreement is brought about by changing people's minds — other people's.*
> *S.I. Hayakawa*

With all that accomplished, now you need to answer one question, What's the goal of your presentation?

- Is it to inform the prospect?
- Is it to introduce your company?
- Is it to introduce your service?
- Is it to get the sale?

I bet you're thinking, "To Get the Sale." But, not every presentation's goal is to walk away with a closed sale. Sometimes, providing all the data about your company, your service, the industry, the need for your service, **and** asking for the sale is just too much for the prospect to absorb. (You'll know they are overwhelmed by the way their eyes glaze over and they try to suppress the yawns.) Before your meeting, ask yourself these questions:

1. Have I met with this person before?
2. Have they met with any of my competitors before?
3. Did I meet with this company in the past but with a different person?
4. What do I want to walk away with?
5. What will I settle for?
6. Will this presentation be a step in a longer process or is it the entire process?

With these answers in mind, decide on your goal. If it's to bring home the sale, you'll have an entirely different approach than if it's simply to introduce your service and establish a need in the prospect's mind. Knowing ahead of time what the aim is will better your chances of getting there.

Time Trials

We're all in a race against time, trying to beat out the competition. So when we hear, "I just don't have time to talk to you right now," we can sympathize with the prospect. But it may also be a stall technique.

> *Time is an illusion, lunchtime doubly so.*
> *—Douglas Adams*

A prospect who is really too busy to talk to you is likely to be a prospect who really needs your help. A prospect who is just putting you off may need your help and not even know it. The following responses will help you hurdle the time objection and race on to the presentation:

> *A study of economics usually reveals that the best time to buy anything is last year.*
>
> —*Marty Allen*

> I understand you're occupied now. How about tomorrow at 9 AM or would 4 PM be better?
>
> I know you are busy, that's why I've condensed my presentation. I'm able to show you how our service will help you in just three points. Let's run through it now.
>
> I agree, time is important. That's why I won't waste yours. I'll get right to the facts of how my service will make your ______ easier and more profitable.
>
> Of course you're busy—look how successful you are! If you had all sorts of time on your hands you wouldn't need my service!
>
> If a customer came in, would you be too busy to speak with him? I can generate more sales and profits for you just as a customer can. Let me tell you how...
>
> I can see your business is doing great. This discussion can make your business even more successful.
>
> I understand you're busy. I can show you how to make the most of the time you do have.

These simple phrases will defeat the time objection and help you speed to the finish line and win the sale.

Selling Things You Believe In

As a sales professional you know it is difficult for most people to sell something they do not believe in. Assuming that you are one hundred percent behind the products and services that you have in your bag, then a prospect who wants to make comparisons should be comfortable for you and something that you would encourage.

How do you react when your prospect says, "This sounds OK but I need to check around for some other companies' rates"? Do you panic? Try to change the subject? There's no reason to see this objection as an obstacle. If you believe in your product, you will have no problem showing your prospect that your service is worth the price. Here are some examples of what you might do:

> *Nothing will ever be attempted if all possible objections must first be overcome*
> *—Dr. Samuel Johnson*

- ☛ "That's a great idea! You should be as informed as possible."
- ☛ "That's great! You'll see that we have the best value."
- ☛ "Great! You'll find out just how much you'll save with us."
- ☛ "You probably see what a value our service is. I have a merchant who used to use company X. He was paying $XX per month before he came on board with us!"
- ☛ "You should know what else is out there. Be sure to include the lost revenue for waiting to make a decision, or the likelihood that the competition may want a longer term commitment."

If your prospect wants to check out other rates, encourage them to do so. Then, focus on the value of your products or services!

"We will begin by reviewing your bankcard sales."

Cartoon by Bradford Veley, Marquette, MI

How to Identify the Prospect's Achilles Heel

What it's going to take to motivate a prospect to buy from you is not always obvious. Less experienced sales representatives often think that it is simply a question of price. The truth of the matter is that price is seldom the stumbling block to closing a sale. Generally the cause is the prospect's resistance to being forced to make a decision.

Without resistance to buying, there would be no need for sales representatives and little need for a sales profession. While the lack of sales resistance may give a stronger feeling of security, resistance remains the most important hurdle every salesperson has to get over, under, or around.

Some successful salespeople actually call objections "the salesperson's best friend." Although this may sound a little ridiculous, they point out that until you know what's keeping a prospect from buying, you can't bring up the right benefits and proofs to minimize the resistance and lead the way to the sale.

Write it Down

Planning is good. We can all agree on that. But, don't become so focused on your presentation that you don't retain what the prospect tells you.

To get in the habit of really listening and remembering what the prospect says, take notes during your conversation. Jot down a few key points the merchant makes, and if the prospect mentions anything more than once, definitely write that down. What you have to say may be important to you, but that doesn't mean it's important to your prospect. It's only important to him if you make it relate to what he's told you.

On the other hand, what the prospect has to say is important to him and even more important to you. He is the one who can tell you how to get the sale. You just need to listen to the clues and write them down.

Put Your Best Foot Forward

You've made presentations hundreds of times and could probably do them in your sleep, right? So who needs help with their presentation? We all do!

First, are you encouraging questions? Great! But, go a step further and ask for them, and not just at the end of your presentation. Tell the merchant to interrupt you whenever a question or a point of procedure needs to be clarified. That way, your prospect is involved in your presentation, and it becomes interactive. If questions still aren't being asked, go ahead and ask them yourself. For example, try saying, "You may be wondering how the Multiple Check Premium would work for you if you had a consumer come in today who didn't have enough money for a down payment." And then explain how it works.

> *The pursuit of perfection often impedes improvement.*
> *—George Wil*

Second, don't be afraid to stress your important points. Have you ever seen a commercial over and over, yet you don't know what it's advertising? Then one day, WHAM, you know its perfume or jeans. We all know the average consumer must see an ad a number of times before being motivated to a buying decision. Therefore, don't be afraid to repeat your important points during your presentation. Pick two or three points you really want to get across, such as "Equipment Reliability" or "24-hour customer service," and mention those throughout your presentation.

Next, honesty really is the best policy. Don't tell a merchant something just because you know it's what he wants to hear. Stick to the facts, remain honest, and you won't have to worry that what you told this person is different from what you told another. Focusing on honest business practices will allow you to make the most sales and have the most satisfied customers. On the same note, if you don't know the answer to a question, don't muddle your way through. Admit you aren't certain of the answer, but make a commitment to find the answer ASAP.

Fourth, if you get nervous, use that energy to your advantage. Channel your adrenaline and harness your anxiety to add enthusiasm to your presentation.

Finally (at the risk of sounding like your mother), "Stand up straight!" Good posture will add credibility to you and your service. Show your prospect that you're proud to represent your company, have faith in your service, and are confident in your own selling skills.

There's always room for improvement, and if you follow these steps, you'll be that much closer to perfect. After all, learning to be a better sales professional is not like learning to be tall. Selling is not acting; it does not exceed the realm of possibility. It just requires practice.

How to Use Your Presentation to Find the Resistance

However you feel about objections, you must know that it's better to avoid them than to overcome them later. That's why professional salespeople plan their presentations to include the answers and proofs they have found will decrease their typical prospect's resistance. Here are some ways to gather and present this information.

Record your most typical objections. Don't trust your memory. Keep a written list of the objections you have dealt with before, and ask your service provider for help with the problem questions.

> *A champion views resistance as a gift of energy.*
> —*Michael J. Gelb*

The best way to avoid resistance from prospects is to anticipate their objections. And why not take advantage of the experience of others in your field? Other salespeople are excellent sources for this kind of information.

Work these benefits and proofs into your sales presentation. If you've discovered that your prospects frequently ask about the size of the negative file that will be used for approval, you might say, "Wouldn't you agree that more sales are more valuable than more declines?" Or if the price of your bankcard services is often cited as above the market, you might say, "Would you agree that good support and 24 hour equipment replacement has more value than pennies saved in monthly fees?"

Set up your strategy so you will be able to handle the objections not easily eliminated in your presentation. To accomplish this, be ready to use testimonials and specific cases that support your service and prove to your prospect that a possible objection is not valid. For example, "Mr. Anderson of Anderson Auto Supplies thought that the price was the most important thing to him, but once he used our service, he found that more approvals created more income. In addition, he found that although overall he paid more than with his previous service provider, it was well worth the gain in profits."

You can't expect to eliminate every objection that a customer raises. You can be sure of closing more sales faster and easier if you take a little time to plan for objections, and watch for the opportunity to close.

Do's and Don'ts

- ✔ Don't open up with "How are you today?" This blares "salesperson."

- ✔ Do identify yourself professionally. Give your name and company name. State the purpose of your call, plus a few brief benefits of your service

- ✔ Don't just send information to the gatekeeper. Say that in order to send the proper information, you must learn a little about the organization and that a brief conversation with the prospect would make that possible. Or ask permission to question the screener on a few points; make the screener feel important.

- ✔ Do treat the gatekeeper with the same professionalism and friendly manner you would your prospect.

- ✔ Do ask to make an appointment to phone your prospect. If the gatekeeper likes you and sees a benefit in allowing you through, a phone appointment can work.

Savvy Sales Tips

The following is a list of successful selling tips.

1. Customers love choices—Visa, MasterCard, Discover, Debit, Purchase, Lease. Avoid dictating the terms of a sale to prospective customers. When choices are offered to customers, it gives them a feeling of empowerment that can help close a deal.

2. Learn customers' views of your competition—Salespeople who actively solicit information from customers about the company's competitors may get early warnings of competitors' bright new products, services, and marketing innovations.

3. Stick to the straight and narrow—It's NOT OK for sales reps to lie, even a little. This extends to exaggerating, omitting key information, and expressing wishful thinking as a fact. It's better to establish trust and risk losing one particular sale than to lie to a customer and risk losing that prospect forever, and anyone he or she may talk to.

Ask Pointed Questions for Specific Answers

When you are meeting with a prospect, do you ask questions such as: Are you satisfied with your current bankcard processor? Is there anything that you want done differently? Is there anything I can do to help you? If you are using questions like these and not getting the information you need, it's because the questions are too open-ended.

Asking vague questions allows your prospect to think that you have all the time in the world to listen to their business problems. It also leads to generalizations, not the specifics you can use to lead the prospect to the buying decision. If the prospect doesn't perceive a problem with the *status quo,* you have no additional information. You need to formulate these questions in a way that helps your prospect focus on the benefits you have to offer.

Start by listing all of the possible loss situations the prospect might encounter without your services. Then formulate questions that best describe these scenarios. For example, instead of saying, "Are you happy with your current check service?" try saying, "How many sales have you lost because your customer's check was not approved?" The table below lists some other pointed questions you might try during your next presentation.

Loss Situation	**Probing Question**
Not enough cash today	How often do you lose a sale when the cus tomer won't have the required cash until "next week?"
No second ID for a check	Do you lose sales when the customer doesn't have the ID required by your current check company?
Claim problems	Does your current check company offer "No Fault" claims?
Time consuming, complicated approval process	Are your customers aggravated at the point-of-sale by your check approval process?

Loss Situation	Probing Question
Bank fees for bad checks	Does your current check company reimburse you for the bad check fees you pay to your bank?

After you have listened to your prospect's answers to these questions, you will be able to highlight your service's benefits. Your prospect will appreciate your knowledge of his or her business. The value of what you have to offer will be tangible to your prospect as you focus in on the business benefits you have available.

Remember: You can hit the sales bull's-eye more often with a pointed question than with a scattered thought.

Talking With a Smile

> *Luck is not chance.*
>
> *It's toil. Fortune's expensive smile is earned.*
>
> *— Emily Dickinson*

Telemarketers and TeleSales professionals must rely solely on their speaking skills to make positive first impressions on their prospects. The standard first impression makers, a professional appearance and eye-catching handouts, aren't available over the phone, and even the most powerfully drafted phone script needs an eloquent and polished delivery to be effective.

The manner in which you speak over the phone conveys 85 percent of your message. Here are some hints to help get your point across smoothly and powerfully.

Answer your phone with a smile in your voice. If you answer your phone rudely, only to quickly adopt a warm, friendly tone of voice, you risk sounding phony. Always use your best phone voice—you never know when your most important prospect may call.

Speak slowly and clearly. Your prospects need more time to absorb what you're saying over the phone than in person. Speak carefully when saying your name and the company name. When leaving a message, be sure to repeat your name and number.

Use body language. Your prospect can't see you, however, your body language translates over the phone through your voice. Physical animation adds animation to your voice, which makes you more engaging. A friendly, welcoming tone will make your prospects warm up to you and your message.

Smile. A smile translates into a pleasant voice, which will hold your prospects' interest more easily than a monotone. Place a mirror in front of you as you speak with prospects, smile as you speak with the person on the other end of the line. Smiling will cause you to speak with more personable tones that will make your message easier to listen to.

Be careful with first names. Always ask if you may use your prospect's first name. Some people are easily offended by others who take the liberty of addressing them by their first name.

Put your enthusiasm in your voice. Without raising your voice, practice speaking so that your prospects get as excited about why you're calling as you are. Be sure to avoid the "pre-school teacher" syndrome—speaking in the soprano register. Aim to modulate your voice at the pitch of "middle C." Don't be afraid to speak in a lower tone than usual. A lower voice is much more pleasant than a high pitched one.

Listen. Don't perfect your speaking skills only to lose the sale with rudeness. No one likes being interrupted. Focus your attention on your prospects—in order to sell to them, you have to listen to their needs. Remember, you're engaged in a two-way conversation, and listening to your prospect is your number one priority.

Concentrate on what your prospect is saying. Don't plan your next words while your prospect is speaking. Ask questions that force you to concentrate on the answer, and show the prospect that you're interested in her needs.

> *People want economy, and they'll pay any price to get it.*
>
> *—Lee Iacocca*

Treat numbers with care. When speaking numbers, go slowly, don't say "o" when you mean, "zero". Being precise will decrease errors. Read numbers back to verify accuracy, and ask to have them read back to you. Take notes. Write things down that you need to remember from the conversation. Before hanging up, review these points with your prospect. Reiterate any agreements, such as your next planned discussion or any figures you have quoted. End your conversations as pleasantly as you begin them.

Strong speaking skills can determine whether your sales will stagnate or skyrocket. With careful practice, your voice can become your greatest asset.

Don't forget, smile, talk happy, and it will mean $$$$s to you.

Key to Selling Value

If you are a Sales Manager, you have heard your sales representatives at some time say, "We're getting beat on price" or "Our customers are making price-based decisions because we haven't elevated those value-based decisions." Perhaps if you're a sales representative yourself, you have even turned these thoughts over in your own head.

But what the pricing issue really boils down to is sales representatives selling to the wrong people. Instead of getting to the person who is empowered to buy value, sales representatives are selling to product evaluators who get paid to assess product, price, service, and delivery and that's all.

When you're selling value, you want to be face-to-face with someone who can say yes when everyone else says no. Those people are the true decision-makers.

John Castle, an ISO in York, PA, illustrates the point this way: "My first and only approach is, 'cost vs. return.' Electronic bankcard processing is a money maker. I show the prospect that it is a profit center. I never sell monthly payment, equipment, or discount rates. I use the tax expense, write-offs, and cost-of-doing-business approaches.

"When I run into a local bank that has the edge and is using a bank relationship to hold their customer, giving the store away, or confusing the prospect, I keep it simple for the prospect.

"The main thing that gets the prospect's attention, from my point of view, is the difference between credit or debit and check guarantee, and how the prospect can make and save money at the same time."

Chapter 9

Closing

Closing Ability Separates the Successful from the Unsuccessful

Closing is the natural conclusion of a well-handled sale, yet it is often seen as an anxiety-laden moment of truth. Here are some observations to help you anticipate closing as a logical, reasonable, and achievable step in the selling sequence.

> *Effective sales always means asking the right question*
> *—Robert Heller*

Your closing attitude affects your performance. Your emotional state will show during a presentation. If you are nervous or face the close with dread, your emotions can jeopardize your sale. Your prospect will perceive your emotions as a lack of confidence or honesty. Viewing your close as a golden opportunity positively influences your prospect. If your emotional state is that of self-confidence, your positive close will be enhanced by your up-beat attitude.

A successful close is simply the last logical step in a long process of carefully planned and executed events. You should anticipate the final close as the payoff on your entire effort.

Closing begins with your initial contact with the prospect. Don't associate "closing" exclusively with the end of the sales process. Closing is an integral part of the entire selling process, not a separate event tacked on to the end. Begin closing as soon as your sales opportunity begins.

A successful sales process contains many preliminary closes. Salespeople must close prospects to set appointments, agree on the prospect's needs, and decide which program best meets those needs. Keep a clear memory of your successful preliminary closes to help boost your confidence when it's time to ask for the order.

Each point of agreement between you and the buyer takes you closer to the successful buying decision. Remember that each point of agreement simplifies the prospect's final decision to buy. Review each point of agreement as you wrap up your presentation.

Allay your prospects' buying anxiety by reviewing the benefits of what they are buying from you. Use your close to make sure you've addressed all objections and concerns, then ask for the sale. Your positive attitude will help the prospect feel comfortable about the decision.

Make closing an eagerly anticipated opportunity to meet your goals!

Decisions That Lead to a Close

Prior to converting a prospect to a customer, four decisions must be made in your favor, culminating in the decision to buy. If you build your presentation to lead the prospect through this decision making process, you will close more sales and make more money. Enable your prospects to decide:

- I need this service.
- I'll do business with you.
- The price is right.
- The time is now.

Need

The first step in any sales process is to enable the prospect to perceive a need for your product. In the financial services marketplace this can often be accomplished by showing merchants how your product will increase their sales. Check guarantee, bankcard, and debit card acceptance are all plus sales opportunities for retail merchants. Show them how this works.

You

> *There are no traffic jams when you go the extra mile.*
>
> — *Anonymous*

After you've defined "The Need," your next step is to convince merchants that you have the answer. With more than 4,000 ISOs vying for your sale, how do you set yourself apart from the crowd? You can offer merchants a faster approval process, guaranteed leasing, an electronic floor plan, or 24-hour customer service. Perhaps you can speak their language—this can mean anything from brushing up on your high school Spanish to learning to speak techno-ese. Find some way to set yourself apart from the crowd by offering more, better, faster.

Right

In a commodity marketplace, convincing merchants that your price is right can be your biggest challenge. Unbundling your products and services can enable you to do this and at the same time make more money. As an ISO, you can fill your black bag with the best programs available.

Now

Since you've already established this plus sales opportunity, it's simple to show merchants that Time = Money. Signing now will lead to more sales now (and if you can program the terminal now, all the better).

Plan your pitch so that merchants say, **"I need you right now."**

Make Sales Easy!

Quick! Name one thing you can do that will absolutely, positively, better your chances of closing a sale? You can make it easy for the prospect to say yes!

Remember, it is in your prospect's job description to make these decisions. And, as we all know, everyone wants his or her job to be easier. So if you can make it simple for the prospect to sign with you instead of someone else, you'll be ahead of the game.

Well how do you make it easy? You can:

Be Prepared. Provide all the papers, brochures, and agreements necessary. If you are up against someone who has only verbally quoted rates, while you've typed up a document with the rates included, you will get the sale. Remember, your decision-maker probably needs to have something to show the boss. Your rates in black-and-white are a lot better than someone else's verbal numbers, even if they're lower.

Be Accessible. Provide your prospect with your phone number, fax number, and mobile number. And don't forget e-mail! Also, schedule a time that's best to reach you. Better yet, make an appointment and you call him at a specific time.

Handle all the Details. Don't leave any loose ends. If something needs to be clarified confirmed, or double-checked, you do it. If someone else needs to be consulted, you do the footwork.

Provide a scenario. Give a vivid, detailed example of an exact instance when your service will be needed and how the prospect will be relieved that she chose to sign with you. Be sure to include how your service makes her job easier.

It is your job to make the prospect's job easier. If two products are up against each other and one has hoops to jump through while the other is simple, you know which one you would pick!

Buying Motivation & Goals

People who need to purchase something are often not motivated to do so because they are:

Unaware that they really need what you have to sell

Suspicious

Resistant to change

Reluctant to spend money

You can motivate them to buy by using your sales skills effectively:

1. Help them identify, verify, and prioritize their needs,

2. Create an open, trusting, problem-solving environment,

3. Show them how your solutions can meet their needs, and

4. Show them why your solutions are cost-effective.

We've all been in a selling situation, certainly as a buyer if not as a seller. As a prospective buyer of clothing, a car, or records, you have probably had to deal with a sales rep. You may have worked as a store clerk, or you may have sold lemonade as a child. We are always being presented with opportunities to buy or sell. Sometimes the final decision is to buy, sometimes it's not. Why?

The following chart shows why people do and do not buy. Notice how basic the reasons are. Sometimes the difference between a close and a "maybe later" is very simple!

Why People Buy	**Why People Do Not Buy**
Trusted the salesperson	Didn't trust the sales person
Felt the salesperson listened	Felt the salesperson didn't really care about me
The sales rep presented himself professionally	The sales rep seemed sloppy
Like the way the rep spoke	The rep seemed uneducated
Showed me the benefits of what she was selling	Didn't seem to know what she was talking about
Answered my questions	Didn't have any answers to my questions or concerns
Took time to explain	Was impatient
Seemed natural	Seemed to be reading from a script
Friendly	Unfriendly
Knowledgeable	Didn't make sense
Enthusiastic	Seemed tired and bored

Too Many Decision Makers

It is imperative to find out who the decision-maker is early in your prospecting. If you aren't talking to the person with the power to say "Yes," you're wasting your breath.

If you ask your prospect if he is the decision-maker and he says, "I'm one of them," do you panic? Do you abandon ship because it will be just too hard to convince a group of people to purchase your product? Don't! Just because you need to get the "Yes" from a group of people rather than one, doesn't mean it will be harder. It's still just one "Yes" and you still need to overcome the same obstacles.

1. First, find out the names of the players and what they do, so you can make your product attractive to each person. For example, the manager will be happy that close outs are easier, the salesperson will be attracted that the checkout time is faster, and the owner may be attracted to the lower cost of the equipment.

2. Next, make sure you notice how each person is introduced and addressed. Find out if the company uses last names or only first names and follow their protocol. Remember, the same rules may not apply to the boss as apply to everyone else. For example, maybe everyone uses his or her first name except for the boss.

3. Next, find out who is boss of whom. Knowing who has the power in the organization will help you if two of the decision-makers have opinions that conflict.

4. Along the lines of number two, you will need to find out the history of the decision-makers. The person highest on the totem pole isn't necessarily the one who has all the clout. Watch for human dynamics. If everyone agrees with the boss, you know who you need to convince.

5. Next, make certain you find out about any decision-makers who are not present. Get their names and positions and see if you can find out why they're not present. Try to get something to them in writing.

6. Find out what each person wants, and be sure to ask questions of the quietest member. If anyone is too quiet, he or she may have concerns that will not be voiced until you leave. Make sure you hear all objections before the group meets without you.

When it comes to presenting your service to a group of people, you don't need to be a psychology major, just be observant. People watching can yield many clues as to how to play the situation and get the sale.

I'm Only Human

Decision-makers have the interests of their business at heart, but that doesn't mean they're not human. Treat them as individuals and you'll get further in your efforts.

> *It is impossible to persuade a man who does not disagree, but smiles.*
>
> *—Muriel Spark*

Think about it. You're a salesperson. How does it feel to know that the person you are talking to is silently thinking, "Salespeople are pushy. They look out for number one. They'll do anything for a sale-maybe ethical, maybe not"? That doesn't feel good, does it? But are you guilty of doing the same to prospects? Are they all "rude," "ignorant" and "self-absorbed"? Give your prospective customers the respect of recognizing that they are more than a list of adjectives commonly attached to certain titles. Approach your prospect as a person, not just as the "sales manager," "owner," or "accountant."

It's important to recognize that people don't really care what you have to say until they feel they can trust your motivation and judgment. Therefore, your first hurdle as a professional salesperson is to set your prospects at ease. If they are to become buyers. they must know that they are putting their money and faith in a worthy company and that the relationship will get even better over time.

In order to build this trust, you, as the sales professional, must be able to offer advice that is good for this person, not just for your commission. You must also provide a variety of solutions and hopefully at least one will involve acquiring your service.

Treating your prospects as people will result in successful closes, quality accounts, and increased referrals.

Closing A Sale

On average it takes seven contacts to make a sale. This is because making a sale isn't just supplying a product or service, but rather gaining the prospect's trust.

When your product or service is offered by other companies, you must win sales by showing your prospects that they can trust you to act in their interest. Most people will make their buying decision based on who you are, not the company you represent.

In order to win this trust, you must be willing to answer all of the prospect's questions and resolve his/her objections. Even when the prospect asks questions that are clearly answered in your literature or when the questions become repetitive, remain calm and courteous. Provide all the answers and explanations the prospect requires. Here are some ideas on the steps in the process.

1. Do you need to meet in person or will a phone call close the deal? You will have to gauge the prospect to make this determination. When an in-person meeting is required. you will want to turn phone inquiries into personal appointments.

2. When you are returning phone calls, be sure to ask if this is a good time to talk—even when you are calling to set up a personal meeting. Try to answer any preliminary questions without going into detail, and never quote a price over the phone when more information is required to establish which service will best meet the prospect's needs. When answering the prospect's questions, emphasize that you will be able to explain everything in detail at your scheduled appointment.

3. Focus on meeting your prospect's needs, not on making the sale. Find out as much as possible about what the prospect needs and then explain how your service can best meet those needs.

4. Understand your service, but more importantly, understand how it fits in with your prospect's business. When the prospect starts asking you questions about the details of your service, don't just plunge into an explanation. Instead, ask probing questions to determine the prospect's exact needs and how you can best serve them. For example, when the prospect asks, "How much will the equipment cost?" don't explain all of the various options. Instead ask, "Will I be setting up one location or more? What are your current procedures? Will you need a cash drawer?" This will give you a much better idea of how to sell your solution.

5. Know what sets you apart from your competition. Never denigrate the other companies in the industry. Instead, know what sets you apart, what you do best, and how what you offer will better meet your prospect's needs.

6. Be confident in yourself and your service. In order for others to trust you, you must believe in what you are doing. Never bluff the answer to a question. If you don't have an answer, do your research and get back to the prospect. Learn everything you can about the product or service you offer and exude this confidence in your speech, attire, posture, and presentation. Show the prospect that you are an expert in your field by answering all of his/her objections and detailing how your service will best meet the prospect's business needs.

7. Offering a guarantee to your prospects will eliminate many objections. Never offer a guarantee you can't deliver, but use the guarantees you have to clinch the sale.

8. Greet your prospect's objections as opportunities. If the prospect is formulating objections, it means that the decision process is still in gear. Objections give you the chance to learn the prospect's thinking process and to further define the prospect's needs. Translate the prospect's objections into questions—especially when dealing with price objections. When the prospect says, "That's too much money," hear, "Is this really going to be worth it?" Ask, "How much is too much?" This will give you a chance to further outline the benefits of the service. Listen to the prospect's objections carefully to determine if you can meet his/her needs. If the service is not what the prospect needs, cut your losses and get out then, rather than later. (Too many sales professionals under-value their time.)

9. Ask if the prospect is ready to make the buying decision. After making your presentation ask, "Does this sound like something you would be interested in?" Asking this type of question should bring out the last of the prospect's objections or show you that this prospect is ready to buy. Don't waste your valuable time continuing to pitch to someone who isn't going to buy.

> *I don't know the key to success, but the key to failure is trying to please everybody.*
> *—Bill Cosby*

10. Ask for the order. Many sales professionals forget to close with the simple, "Shall we finish up the paperwork now? Would you like to start this afternoon or tomorrow morning? Establishing our service takes about 10 minutes, shall we program your terminal now?" Don't lose all of the momentum of your sales presentation by forgetting to ask for the sale.

11. Get the signature. No deal is closed until the money is in hand or the signature is on the dotted line. Don't leave the sale open with promises to finish up later. Complete the paperwork now.

12. If you can't close the sale, leave the door open. If you find out that the person you've pitched doesn't have signature authority, or is unable to make a commitment now, don't close the door on future opportunities. Set a specific date for a follow-up call. Get the name of the decision-maker. Send a thank you and follow-up material, and calendar your meeting or follow-up call.

Seven Buying Signals, Do You Recognize Them?

Some prospects send buying signals which should point you towards the commitment process and "the close." These buying signals are often in the form of questions which show that the prospect is leaning in your direction.

Here are some common buying signals.

1. The prospect asks questions about how long it takes to establish the service. "How long does it take to program my terminal?" or "When could I begin guaranteeing my checks?"

2. The prospect asks about payment terms or policies. "Are your invoices standard net 30?" or "With your RCK service, when will I get paid?"

3. The prospect asks specific questions about the service details. "How does the Pre-Auth courtesy work?" or "What information does my sales-staff need to put on the check?"

4. The prospect begins making positive statements of agreement. "This service really could save me a lot of money in return check fees."

> *He that speaks ill of the mare will buy her.*
> *— Benjamin Franklin*

5. The prospect becomes more at ease with the conversation.

6. The prospect begins speaking about how his or her company would use the service. "This debit process would really speed things up at the register and simplify our non-credit process."

7. The prospect begins to negotiate price. "How much would my charge be per check with the multiple check option and without?"

When your prospect begins to ask some of these questions, your sales professional's instinct should tell you that it's time to begin "the close." You can do this by moving to one of your standard closes or by asking more questions to help the prospect sell himself; for instance, "What is it you like best about our proposal?"

By learning to recognize buying signals you will know when to move forward toward the close, and be able to move more quickly to the next prospect.

Offensive Silence

One of the sales professionals' most useful skills is his mastery of the power of silence. It is a skill applied in two modes: defensive silence and offensive silence. Defensive silence is a deliberate, focused silence which allows the salesperson's intense concentration on what the customer is saying and a more accurate interpretation of what the customer's words and inflections mean. Offensive silence is a disciplined resistance to saying more than is necessary to close the order. These two distinctly different and important applications of the power of silence, properly executed, will produce far greater results than any amount of practice and refinement of presentation skills.

Although a meeting between a salesperson and a prospective buyer is, by definition, the salesperson's opportunity to present a product or service for the customer's consideration, in reality, the more the customer talks, the greater control the salesperson has over the outcome of the meeting. He allows the customer to talk himself into the sale.

J. Douglas Edwards, one of the finest sales and management trainers in the country, sums up his lecture on the art of closing with a demonstration of what he calls "the single most important instruction" he will ever give his audience. He begins softly,

"Whenever you ask a closing question," then screams at the top of his lungs, "SHUT UP AND LISTEN!" Those of us who have been jolted out of our seats become instant believers.

The learned skill of "shutting up" is applicable throughout the sales process. Very often a salesperson will hear the first few words of a customer's objection (one so often repeated and familiar that the salesperson could answer it in his sleep) and cannot resist the urge to interrupt the customer.

"I know, but check guarantee is really cheaper than verification, if you will just let me show you!"

Had the salesperson shut up, very likely the customer would have answered or dismissed the objection out of hand, "With verification, I was still responsible for the bad checks. What good is that?"

Sometimes the customer's expanded remarks reveal a deeper, hidden objection, one that will remain forever hidden if the salesperson interrupts. Interruptions are rude and disrespectful, and do not endear the salesperson to the customer.

The art of being silent is, by itself, more powerful than all other selling skills combined. While it is possible to earn a living and even build a successful career without mastering this skill, the selling life is certainly easier and more productive for those who do.

Learn to Love Objections

We all face objections, the key is turning them into selling opportunities.

As you know, an objection is better than a simple "No" because it opens up an opportunity for dialogue. Another great thing about objections is that the same ones come up over and over. That means you have ample opportunity to prepare your solution and take up **ARMS.**

> **A**nticipate objections. Anticipating gives you time to prepare answers before you meet with the prospect.
>
> **R**ephrase objections. Rephrasing verifies that you understand the objection, lets your prospect know that you're listening, and gives you time to formulate your rebuttal. It also helps you discover the real objection. When you hear an objection that doesn't make sense, rephrasing it can force the prospect to clarify.
>
> **M**ake certain you hear every objection. Trust your intuition. If you feel there is something holding the prospect back, there probably is. Don't avoid that unspoken objection. Ask what it is; otherwise, it will stand in the way of the sale.
>
> **S**how your prospects that you understand their objections, and more importantly, their position. If you can demonstrate that you understand their perspective, you will increase their trust in you and the credibility of your service. If you don't understand an objection, ask the prospect why he has a particular objection. If he can't state why he feels a certain way, the objection doesn't really exist. If he can explain his feelings, you are better equipped to dismiss it and close the sale.

It doesn't have to be a battlefield out there. Just be prepared.

"Learning to love objections means not letting them push your buttons."

Cartoon by Bradford veley, Marquette, MI

Another Kind of Objection

Being in an industry with several service providers can be good for the industry because the competition promotes increasingly better services. But it can also be detrimental to your selling efforts when the proverbial bad apple spoils the bunch. What do you do when you're met with the following?

"No thanks. We used company X and it wasn't for us."

"We used a service like yours and it was a waste of time."

"We tried something like that before, and the company still owes us money. No thanks!"

How do you differentiate your service when your prospect has a preconceived notion of what your service is and does? How do you separate your company from those that offer similar products, especially to merchants who have used other services previously?

Look for ways in which your service is different from your competitors'—and stress them. For example:

Have you been in business longer?

Do you specialize in certain merchant types or industries?

Have you received any awards or publicity?

What specific services make you unique? (Multiple check, sales saver, premium approval...)

Apply the merchant's thinking to another industry. For example, all car companies manufacture cars, but that doesn't mean all cars are the same. Many companies offer phone service, but consumers definitely have their favorites.

Stressing the diversity within your industry can help your prospect see how unique your company is and what you can offer that your competitors cannot.

Chapter 10

Starting The Cycle Over

After the Appointment

How did you fare at your last appointment? Whether you closed the sale or not, see if you hit these important points:

> *The toughest thing about success is that you've got to keep on being a success.*
> —*Irving Berlin*

1. Did you talk less than a quarter of the time?

2. Did you focus on results?

3. Did you find out what the prospect wants from your type of service?

4. Did you find out how the prospect could benefit from your service?

5. Did you ask the most important question, **did you ask for the sale?**

No matter how your appointment ended, hit these points and you'll have a better grasp of the merchant's needs and how you can position your service to fill those needs next time.

The Time Before Time

What's the timeline of your sales presentations? Do you go to a prospect, present your service, get the sale (or not), and then move on to the next conquest? Remember, the time after an appointment is just as important as the time before. And, if you didn't get the sale, the time after is even more important.

Regardless of the outcome of the meeting, always take time to review what happened. As difficult as it may be to relive the trauma, you can use all your experiences, even the negative ones, to push you toward more sales. If you didn't get the sale, don't get discouraged. Remember, for every "No," you're a bit closer to a "Yes!" Think about it: if it takes 20 prospects to get one sale, every prospect who says "No" is nudging you closer to that one who will say "Yes!" Analyze what transpired and try to define the moment when the rejection solidified in your prospect's mind.

Most importantly, try to learn something new every day. At the end of each day, take the time to replay your day and find at least one thing you've learned that will make your selling efforts even better tomorrow.

Dear Diary

You probably already keep a schedule of your sales appointments and results of calls, but try and go a little further. Keep a daily journal of your sales activities and accomplishments.

Record what you do prior to the sales call: how you locate a prospect, what happens at the sales call, the time it took to accomplish each task, and the goals you achieved as well as the ones you need to work on. Include objections heard, closes used, results yielded, and your state of mind. Try to be as specific as possible.

Get in the habit of recording this data daily. After a few weeks, review your journal and look for patterns that led to success and those that did not. Adapt your selling efforts to reflect your positive closes.

You may not think your journal is interesting reading, but it will be profitable to you.

Sales Recycling

If you write detailed bids or proposals for your prospects, what happens to the ones you didn't sign? Instead of wasted paper, these may be a source of potential sales. Are they happy? Did they make the correct decision? Has the person making the original decision left the company?

Keep a file of the "ones that got away," with detailed notes on what they liked about the service, and why they went with the competitor. Then set a follow-up date for several months in the future.

These merchants won't call you—it's too difficult to admit they made a mistake. However, if you call them with, "I just wanted to let you know that we appreciated the opportunity to bid on your business. How is it going with XYZ Company?"

If the merchant raves about his new service provider, reply with a, "Well, that's great."

Don't "bad-mouth" the competition. However, if the merchant should hint at dissatisfaction, probe for more details. Don't assume an "I told you so" attitude rather, become the "problem solver." Empathize with the merchant while you discover exactly what it is that the competition is failing to do. Allow the merchant to save face after making a bad choice.

> *If you have a job without aggravations, you don't have a job.*
>
> *—Malcolm Forbes*

Remember, you must listen carefully to what the prospect is saying, as this may be your second shot at this account.

Call Back Timing

We all know that most of our sales should be a one-call close, and if life were perfect, all of our sales would go that way. Unfortunately, we have to live in the real world. Sometimes we not only can't get an answer on the spot, we can't get to the decision maker because he or she is gone. What do you do upon their return?

I suggest when you have called a prospect and learned that the decision maker will be away for a few days, ask the person you are talking to when he will return. Then don't call on the prospect that day. It's likely that the traveler will return to a mountain of paper work and a logjam of messages requiring action.

I suggest calling several days after his return. You'll have a better chance of reaching the decision maker after he has had time to crawl out from under the accumulated correspondence, and after the "dust has settled."

The prospect will likely be closer to normalcy, and will be in a better position to spend quality time with you. Don't forget to tell him, "Ms. Jones told me that you would be back on Tuesday, so I delayed my call to you to give you a chance to catch up from being away." The prospect should appreciate the fact that you have considered his schedule in your planning.

Avoiding Zero Commission

We all know the saying, "Time is Money." Often sales professionals under value their time. They are afraid to express the fact that they should generally not need to make a second or third sales call, provided they have done their homework to begin with.

The typical problem is price vs. value. A customer may feel the price is just too high for the value they will receive.

Think back, did you present the product in the right light? If you showed the client just how much value he will receive, including you, there's no way he won't buy from you.

Remember: Your time is money, and the commissions you earn on the sales you don't make, are zero.

Overcoming Rejection

So, the last account you sold was signed with a quill pen and your last signed contract was delivered by Pony Express?

OK, maybe it hasn't been that long since you've closed a sale, but it has been a little longer than you'd like.

Don't get down. Rejection is inevitable and there are plenty of other accounts waiting to be sold. They key is not to prevent rejections, the key is to handle them effectively, before and after the presentation.

Before the Presentation

1) **Prepare Prepare Prepare.** It's been drilled into your head, but that's because it's so important.

   ☞ Tape your presentation.

   ☞ Rehearse.

   ☞ Ask others for input.

   ☞ Be prepared for price objections.

   ☞ Find out the merchant's needs and align your service to meet those needs.

2) **Call on prospects who need your service. Don't waste time on unqualified buyers.** Make a list of qualities merchants must have before you will meet with them. (What volume should the business produce, does the business need to be a certain size, are multiple locations an issue, what clientele do they serve, etc.) That way you are in control and, essentially, you can reject them as unqualified before they can reject you.

After the Presentation:

1) **Face the rejection, and move on to your next prospect.** You're not the only person to be rejected and this isn't the last time you will be rejected. Don't be ashamed.

> *Willy was a salesman. And for a salesman, there is no rock bottom to the life. He don't put a bolt to a nut, he don't tell you the law or give you medicine. He's a man way out there in the blue, riding on a smile and a shoeshine.*
>
> *—Arthur Miller*

2) **Use positive self-talk.** This business is demanding and you're doing a great job. Think of all your successes. Use those to motivate you for the next presentation.

3) **Don't dwell.** It's OK to be rejected, just don't let it get in the way of an effective presentation.

4) **Go back to the prospect in a month or so.** Keep trying. A Dartnell study has shown that 95% of the sales professionals surveyed stopped calling on accounts after six "No's" but, in many cases, the "Yes" didn't come until the ninth time!

Learn From Your Mistakes

Each of us makes mistakes, some big and some small. However, repeating mistakes, or failing to learn their lessons, will lead you nowhere. Learning from your mistakes by careful examination of the cause(s) will enable you to improve your overall approach, and keep repeat errors to a minimum.

Here are five steps to analyzing your mishaps, and transforming them into important learning experiences.

1. Research the mistake diligently. The root of a mistake or lost sale may not be what appears most obvious. Uncover every factor that contributed to the problem. The obvious cause may be hiding other factors that need to be addressed.

2. If you lost the sale because you sold the wrong service/platform, you may need an update on the service offerings now in place.

3. Many sales mistakes can be eliminated by annually attending your check or bankcard provider training. Consider calling to register for the next training seminar.

4. Analyze your standard sales approach. Look at your routines, is there a recurring pattern of problems or mistakes? The correction and elimination of mistakes may require a minor (or perhaps major) alteration to your standard sales approach. Perhaps the promises you are making at the time of sale are unrealistic. For instance, promising terminals more rapidly than you can acquire and program them only leads to disappointment on the merchant's side and stress on yours.

5. Confirming your own office equipment inventory or calling your bank service provider before your sales presentation will allow you to confirm which program features and rates are applicable.

Don't get stuck offering what can't be delivered. Review your presentations before you pitch your prospect.

Carry your solutions over to other areas of your business. If your mistake is the result of poor listening skills, practice listening without interrupting during all of your conversations. Poor listening skills can adversely affect your life and business in all areas. Spend more time listening than talking to reduce errors and misunderstandings.

Examine any deviations from your standard sales approach. If "special circumstances" are leading to mistakes, changes in your approach may help eliminate these blunders. Routines are an essential business strategy both to reduce mistakes and to improve efficiency. Once you've established your routines and sales approach, vary from them only when absolutely necessary. Pre-planning your sales calls will help to eliminate misquotes and confusion.

Sales, like life, is all trial and error. After all, it is really what we learn, after we know it all, that really counts.

The Evolving Payment System Sale

Cartoon by Bradford Veley, Marquette, MI

About the Author...

Paul H. Green

Good Selling! draws on Paul Green's 30+ years of sales and marketing experience.

Paul Green is Editor-In-Chief of *The Green Sheet* and *GSQ: The Payment Systems Quarterly*, and is Chief Executive Office of CrossCheck, Inc., the nation's largest independently owned check guarantee company. He is CEO of Concepts, Inc., a leading computer and Internet service company; and CEO/Founder of American Marketing Corporation (AMCOR), the nation's first bankcard Independent Sales Organization. His annual "U.S. Check Study" has become the industry source for tracking trends in checking, and is frequently quoted in trade journals and economics textbooks. Paul was previously president of Telecredit Check Services, Inc., prior to its acquisition by Equifax, and was responsible for that companies 300 million to 3 billion dollars a year growth.

Paul Green holds a BA degree in Accounting and Computer Science, an MBA, and has been a Financial Executive Institute Member for over 20 years. Paul is a noted lecturer, an acclaimed artist and art collector, an amateur classicist and biblical historian, an avid outdoorsman and world-class explorer. Paul has been happily married to his wife, Tischa, for 32 years.

About The Green Sheet

In 1983, after first founding AMCOR, Paul Green recognized there was a rapidly growing, national sales force that needed training and motivation. Thus, *The Green Sheet*, his biweekly motivational newsletter with "actionable advice" for those in the Financial Service Industry, was born. Over the last 16 years, *The Green Sheet* has been evolving with the ISO and is now the only publication for the Financial Services Industry published simultaneously on the Internet and paper.

Features in *The Green Sheet* include business opportunities, information resources, evolving technologies, banking and legal changes, and government issues. The newsletter features The Resource Guide, an advertising section that includes contact information for companies and services vital to the Financial Services industry. *The Green Sheet* also offers sales appropriate articles such as selling tips and motivational information, which continue to be the highest rated information from the Sales Professional's perspective. To further service the ISO, all articles are permanently archived and can be accessed via *The Green Sheet's* web site.

In 1995 *The Green Sheet* became its own independent publishing company, The Green Sheet, Inc., which now publishes the 28-page newsletter, *The Green Sheet*, *GSQ: The Payment Systems Quarterly* magazine, and *The Green Sheet* On-Line (www.greensheet.com). These publications, whether in print or electronic form, are dedicated to serving as a forum where ISOs receive bias-free, timely information relevant to the rapidly expanding financial services market. The Green Sheet, Inc. provides data applicable to all aspects of the market including check verification and guarantee, bankcard and ATM services, debit, credit, EFT, ECP, and Internet commerce.

THE GREEN SHEET, INC.

Do you subscribe to *The Green Sheet?*

Would you like multiple copies of this book

to distribute to your sales force?

Quanitity discounts available.

1st-year Free subscriptions available for

The Green Sheet & **GSQ**.

Contact us at:

800-757-4441

grnsht@aol.com

www.greensheet.com

P.O. Box 6008

Petaluma, CA 94955-6008